Somalia: The Land Of Camel Milk And Honey

Reflections and Recollections of a Time Long Past

By

Steve Tunnicliffe

Copyright © 2023 by – Steve Tunnicliffe – All Rights Reserved.

It is not legal to reproduce, duplicate, or transmit any part of this document in either electronic means or printed format. Recording of this publication is strictly prohibited.

All of the photographs in this book are copyright © David R. Tunnicliffe. All rights reserved.

"There is hope after despair and many suns after darkness."

— Molānā Jalāl ad-Dīn Muḥammad Rūmī

Dedication

This book is dedicated to my Mum and Dad, who took our family to Somalia, and to my wife, Joanne, for her enduring love and encouragement.

Acknowledgement

Writing a book is harder than I thought and more rewarding than I could have ever imagined. I first started making notes and an outline in 2019 when making many long-haul flights either Transatlantic or to the Middle East and Africa. It was only after reading Tim Hannigan's books *The Granite Kingdom* and *The Travel Writing Tribe* that I finally pulled my finger out and started to pull my "etchings" together into something that roughly looked like a book! So thank you Tim!

I want to express my gratitude to my parents, David and Anthea, for taking me and my siblings, Georgina and Richard, to Somalia. This experience has been incredibly formative for all of us. Indeed, a big thank you to my Dad, David, for allowing me to use his beautiful images in this book. *Mahadsanid Daoud!*

I want to express my heartfelt gratitude to my wife, Joanne, and our daughters, Alexa and Antonia, for their unwavering support and encouragement throughout the journey of completing this book. A special thank you goes to Joanne for her invaluable role as my voice of reason and sound judgment.

About the Author

Steve Tunnicliffe has spent much of his life living and working in the Middle East and Africa. His first spoken language was not English but Amharic as he spent his early childhood in Ethiopia prior to the Ethiopian Revolution. When his father, David, was appointed as Cultural Attaché at the British Embassy Mogadishu, Steve subsequently lived for two years with his family in Somalia in the early 1980s and travelled extensively in the country.

In the early 1990s, Steve studied for his BA(Hons) degree in Arabic with Middle Eastern and Islamic Studies at Durham University before subsequently completing his MBA at Durham University Business School. Steve has completed dissertations on specialised translation (Arabic to English), *Rihla* travel literature, and new product marketing.

Steve started his career in television working for a leading Middle Eastern broadcaster, MBC Group, where he met his wife. He has subsequently spent the last 23 years working in the satellite communications industry. Steve also holds a Diploma in Corporate Governance from the Corporate Governance Institute.

Steve currently resides in the United Kingdom with his wife, Joanne, and remains passionate about the Middle East and Africa but Somalia in particular. '*The Land of Milk and Honey*' is Steve's first published work.

Table of Contents

Dedication iii
Acknowledgement iv
About the Author v
Map vii
Preface 1
Selected Glossary 4
Introduction 5
Chapter 1 – The Arrival 7
Chapter 2 – A Land of Breathtaking Beauty 14
Chapter 3 – Sunny Days by the Sea 25
Chapter 4 - Walking into a POW camp 34
Chapter 5 - Travelling to Merka 39
Chapter 6 - Travelling to Warsheikh 45
Chapter 7 - Istunka 48
Chapter 8 - Dining Out on the Afgooye Road 56
Chapter 9 - A road trip to Buur Heybe 60
Chapter 10 - Mogadishu Old 69
Chapter 11 - Mogadishu New 78
Chapter 12 - Living on the Afgooye Road 90
Chapter 13 - Visitors 103
Chapter 14 - Farewell 108
Chapter 15 – Afterword 111
Selected Bibliography 117

Map

Preface

There are many excellent books written about Somalia and particularly what has unfolded over there in the last three decades. There has been much carnage, death, and destruction, which has been very visible to the world. Whilst many of the names of the places and cultural references that appear in the news are very familiar, I have found it challenging to relate the images I have in my head of the Somalia today to the Somalia I lived as a child. They are entirely worlds apart in every aspect.

Indeed there is much commentary going on currently (April 2023) about the unfolding events in Sudan and drawing parallels to what unfolded in Somalia some thirty years ago. The desperate events in Sudan have prompted many observers to draw parallels to the turbulent period that Somalia experienced three decades ago. The echoes of history serve as a reminder of the complexities and challenges faced during times of political and social upheaval. As discussions and analysis continue to unfold, the Somali experience offers valuable insights into the dynamics of conflict, the importance of fostering stability, and the imperative of finding sustainable solutions to promote peace and development. By reflecting on Somalia's past, there is an opportunity for collective learning and the application of lessons that can help shape a more peaceful and prosperous future for Sudan and other regions experiencing similar challenges. For me, the parallel begins and finishes with two competing leaders, and again whilst carnage has followed in Sudan, the experience is very different. Somalia and its people have suffered a great deal for many years now.

In writing this book, I take no political position whatsoever. The politics of Somalia then and now is for Somalis and not for me as an outsider to comment on. The reader will, therefore, see little in the way of political comment and any reference to my views on President Mohammed Siad Barre or the government of the time. Neither will the reader see my comment, in any manner, on Somali federalism or clannism. The intent of this book is to just share a Somalia I saw and experienced once.

I was inspired to put pen to paper by reading Gerald Hanley's *Warriors: Life and Death among the Somalis*. It is one of the few books that really capture anything near Somalia I once experienced: *desolate, sun-scorched land inhabited by independent people with all their single-mindedness, vanity, and fierceness.*

Like Hanley this book is a collection of recollections of a time past. When Hanley published his book in the 1970s it was some 25 years after having left Somalia and forty years since he first went to East Africa as a nineteen year old. In my case, whilst I have travelled to East Africa more recently, it is now forty years since I last stepped foot in Somalia.

The reality is that things change and when I looked recently on Google Maps at satellite earth observation images of the Afgooye Road, my old road stretching from Mogadishu to Afgooye, there is nothing that looks remotely familiar. The road and surrounding environs are now densely populated and yet forty years ago it was barren scrub broken up very occasionally by the odd building. I no longer see anything that remotely resembles our home or indeed the much larger structure, my school.

This is perhaps not surprising: At the time of the fall of President Siad Barre on the 27th January 1991 and the disintegration of the Somali state, patterns of residency changed dramatically. At the time I lived in Somalia the population of Mogadishu was just under half a million people. By 1992 the population had grown to in excess of 2 million people due to the mass influx of refugees.

Needless to say, in this book there will be omissions and mistakes. I will also repeat myself - I do that a lot! - and there will be places and events I conflate. But I hope at least I have been able to capture a sense of life at that time and reflect Somalia in an honest and real way.

Rooftop view of Mogadishu

Selected Glossary

Aqal - dwelling

Berkads - pool

Caano iyo malab - milk and honey

Dabshid - fire

Deg yar - Somali breed of goat

Degmada - *district*

Geel - camel

Geelxir - herder

Gurti - house

Hilib Ari Duban - roast goat meat

Istunka - stick fight

Jama'a - mosque

Laambad - stick fight

Liido - lido or seafront - from the Italian

Mahadsanid - thank you

Nadab - peace or hello

Nabad gilyo - goodbye

Neyruz - solar new year

Subax wanaagsan - good morning

Sheekha - sheikh

Warki - news or information

Introduction

Somalia has endured a great deal over the past thirty years, be it politically or economically. The country was immediately thrown into turmoil following the overthrow of President Siad Barre in 1991. Between 1990 and 1992, customary law temporarily collapsed, factional fighting ensued, and it was not long before Somalia turned into a failed state. Sadly this factional fighting created a vacuum that terrorism filled, primarily in the form of Al Shabaab. Whilst the story we hear of Somalia today is far more positive and affirmative, it is still very much in a fragile state with competing forces pushing different agendas backed by foreign state actors. Thirty years have now passed since the Civil War ensued, leaving the country to perpetual infighting, clannism, and turmoil. This picture has not just jeopardized the position of the State globally but has also left the vast majority of the population to suffer the consequences.

Many people who could flee did not waste much time as the state of affairs of their country was quite evident to the general public, and they abandoned Somalia for neighbouring countries, such as Kenya and Ethiopia. While many others left as refugees to Yemen, the United Kingdom, Sweden, and the United Arab Emirates, and indeed, vast numbers of people moved to the United States in an attempt to find a better life. In many ways, they were the lucky ones who lived their lives in freedom despite the significant upheaval and cultural displacement, now observing events unfold in Somalia from afar. Indeed many have formed businesses that continue to trade through familial connections with Somalia. And who knows, the odds may have been in their favour.

The Somali diaspora is estimated to be just over a million people, with the largest clusters of people in the United States and the United Kingdom. The diaspora community, to be unambiguous, is very vibrant and active, on social media and on Twitter in particular! My Dad, David, launched a photographic site dedicated to his Somali images. He wanted to showcase his perspective of Somalia to the rest of the world. He was the British Cultural Attaché to Somalia between 1981 and 1983, and, during that time he was afforded the opportunity to capture many aspects of Somali life in cooperation with the Ministry of Culture. Following the launch of the website, we promoted to a few hundred Somalis with whom we are connected on Twitter, and in a short span of time comprising of a mere few months, it already had over a hundred thousand visitors! This is a clear testament to the deep interest of primarily the Somali diaspora in their heritage, much of which has been destroyed either through the factional fighting of the Civil War or, indeed, by Al Shabaab.

The overwhelming reaction of the Somali diaspora made me question why the interest. I think the answer to that question lies in a sad reality. According to the United Nations World Population Prospects (The 2010 Revision), only 2.7% of the Somali population was over the age of 65 years. The implications of that statistic today in 2023 mean that an extremely small percentage of the population has any memory of Somalia from the 1970s and 1980s. By extension, therefore, interest in Somali culture and heritage, particularly from the pre-Civil War period, is extremely vibrant among Somalis. This observation regarding the demographic composition of the Somali population and its implications for the interest in Somali culture and heritage implies that with a small percentage of the population having direct memory of Somalia from the 1970s and 1980s, it can indeed create a situation where there is a strong desire among Somalis to reconnect with and preserve their cultural roots.

As a non-Somali visitor, I feel very privileged to have lived and experienced Somalia. Rightly many will argue that my view of Somalia is tainted with my preconceived ideas as a white, middle-class, middle-aged British person, and arguably, as a young teenager, many will assert I have rose-tinted spectacles of a country I saw from a position of privilege. However, I mean no harm and greet my Somali readers with *caano iyo malab* (milk and honey). The intent of this book is to intentionally steer away from politics and terrorism and just focus merely on my memories of Mogadishu and Somalia. There are many great books that cover the more turbulent aspect of Somalia's near past and the rise of Al Shabaab that are significantly more adept at setting out a historical and political context than I would wish.

I should point out, however, that the political environment of the early 1980s was by no means plain sailing either! President Siad Barre was fundamentally a military dictator who exercised a very autocratic style of government exercising all the organs of the State, including the sometimes overzealous Somali National Security Service (NSS).

Chapter 1 – The Arrival

"What have I done?" sobbed my Dad irrepressibly. Burying his head in his hands, what appeared to be deep regret poured out of the breakfast table at the Al Uruba Hotel (Al Curuuba Hotal). We had been in Mogadishu for just two days, and already things had not started well. My Mum and we three children looked on as Dad sat there in a state of distress. I was palpably shocked by the episode as I had rarely seen him cry, let alone in such a public setting, and this was an open display of sorrow. For a seasoned traveller who had already spent time in some very complex environments, this was highly unusual. But given the stress of having to relocate from one country to another and with a young family move to a country with many unknowns and uncertainty, his outpouring of emotion was entirely reasonable.

Our journey to Mogadishu was uneventful. We flew overnight from London Heathrow on a British Airways 747 to Nairobi, Kenya, where we stopped over for a few days. We stayed at the Acacia Hotel in downtown Nairobi which was very exciting for us children, but my Dad later remarked that he had opted to stay in a cheaper hotel given the mediocre allowances! The room had a bedside radio which piped into the room a looped Beatles playlist. There is only so much Norwegian Wood that one can listen to! Our forays were limited to the area around the hotel, as this was effectively a brief stopover before our onward journey to Mogadishu. I recall my Dad disappeared for a few hours to make himself acquainted with the staff at the British High Commission, on which we would subsequently become very dependent. Whilst the embassy in Mogadishu was generally self-sufficient, it depended a great deal on a weekly postal service via the Queen's Messenger including medicines, the occasional fresh food and other essential services.

After a day or so, we returned to the airport for our onward flight on Somali Airlines from Nairobi to Mogadishu. The flight was very rudimentary compared to our British Airways flight to Nairobi. The plane was one of three 707s that had a standard orange Boeing livery, and from what I remember all seats were economy class although on one of the aircraft there may have been a very small business class section. As we crossed from Kenya to Somalia, the plane descended to around twenty thousand feet, and we were able to clearly see the beautiful coastline from Kismayo as we headed north.

We arrived in Mogadishu in June 1981. I can remember the doors of the aircraft being opened and the air conditioning instantly evaporating to be replaced by a wall of very warm air. The ambient temperature was around 40 degrees Celsius with slight humidity. The air tasted of salt, which is perhaps not surprising given that we were right on the Indian Ocean.

We were met on the tarmac at the airport by my Dad's predecessor, Peter Westcombe. In those days, there was no such thing as passport control for arriving diplomats. Our passports were handed to the embassy fixer, and our bags were loaded into the office Land Rover directly from the Somali Airlines 707 hold doors before driving up to what would eventually become our new home for welcome refreshments and a quick barbeque. It was clear that the Westcombes were fast packing and closing their sojourn in Mogadishu.

We were then shuttled down to our hotel on the picturesque Liido, the Al Uruba Hotel. I sometimes wonder whether it was an act of "tough love" for the embassy to have us put up in the Al Uruba rather than the more pleasant and Italian run and owed Albergo Croce del Sud, but we were in for an awakening.

The hotel was the main premier Mogadishu hotel and an imposing building of grand Italianate colonial architecture, as a number of notable buildings in the city dating back to Italian colonial occupation in the 1930s, and had a commanding presence in the centre. However, its grandeur was superficial. Everything was rather basic and seemed considerably less polished than the hotel we had just stayed in, in Nairobi en route to Mogadishu. But the staff tried very hard to make our stay comfortable despite the hotel facing the sea, our rooms faced the main thoroughfare in front of the hotel.

The exterior grandeur of the building was truly captivating, standing tall at about four stories high, its architectural beauty accentuated by the brilliant white stucco that adorned its facade. A striking feature, reminiscent of jagged teeth, encircled the top of the structure, adding a touch of uniqueness to its design. While the exterior dazzled under the sun's rays, the interior presented a contrasting atmosphere – subdued and cloaked in darkness. This deliberate design choice sought to cleverly deflect the intense sunlight, ensuring the coolness of the building's inner chambers. The numerous windows facing the sea played a dual role, not only inviting in refreshing sea breezes but also allowing natural light to softly illuminate the otherwise dimly lit interior, creating a serene oasis from the scorching heat outside.

Had the embassy been kinder, where perhaps we should have stayed was the Italian-run Abergo Croce Del Sud (Hotel Southern Cross), run by the Briatte family, who were originally from Padua, rather than the State-run Al Uruba Hotel. The Abergo was a traditionally Italian-run hotel, and any of our visitors were naturally always put up there. The hotel was on a square and the main thoroughfare close to the Catholic cathedral. From the Italianate architecture, you could have easily thought you were in Rome or Milan. The square was surrounded by palms and flame trees, which naturally attracted a variety of bird life.

However, we were put up in the Al Uruba and we were forced out of necessity to make do. Unfortunately, there was an issue with the plumbing, and the toilet in one bedroom drained into the shower plug hole, which was rather unpleasant. Needless to say, we limited our use to our parent's bathroom. The rooms had air-conditioning, but the bedding was basic, consisting of bright white sheets on well-used mattresses.

The only meal we had at the hotel was breakfast. This was an experience. As with everything, breakfast was rather simple, consisting of bread rolls and boiled eggs. This was our first introduction to a beetle friend who would be with us for the next two years, the ever-present weevil. Each morning we would have to scoop out the soft bread finger rolls impregnated with weevils leaving the outer part of the roll to eat. This became a daily pastime at lunch. The boiled eggs were inedible, and a number were seriously off. I do recall my sister who was six at the time cracking her egg open to reveal a cooked chick much to her disgust! In all dining at the hotel was quite an experience and short lived!

My Dad's unusual moment of weakness on day two was met with real stoicism from my Mum, Anthea. Anthea showed in that instant a side of her personality thus far unseen by her children. She commanded in a rather stoic and British stiff upper lip manner, *"Well. We had just better get on with it and make the most of it."* My Dad's act of remorse had instantly been met with forgiveness, and he rubbed his eyes clear of tears and pulled himself together. I should point out that she had already experienced very complex environments "following my Dad," including eighteen months in Saigon just after the bloody Tet Offensive.

Dad had been so excited on hearing of his promotion following a highly productive, busy but short posting to Jeddah, Saudi Arabia, serving under the illustrious gentleman and diplomat Ambassador Sir James Craig. Busy in the sense that the British Embassy in 1980 and 1981 had been dealing with the fallout from the controversial docudrama *Death of a Princess* as well as working hard to support British businesses in securing the first Al Yamamah defence contract that would help bring about modernisation in Saudi Arabia through the connected defence offset programme.

Dad's excitement was palpable as he eagerly anticipated his upcoming promotion and cross-posting "back to Africa". He fondly recounted his previous two-year experience living in Addis Ababa during the early 1970s, a time filled with cherished memories. Drawing upon those African associations, he couldn't help but envision Somalia as a place that might share similarities. Little did he know how mistaken he would be. Prior to departing from Jeddah, he made the bittersweet decision to part ways with his ex-NATO Series 2 Land Rover, a faithful companion throughout his journeys. In its place, he purchased a brand-new Land Rover V8 Long Wheel Base, the embodiment of adventure, and had it shipped directly to his destination. Little did he know that this new vehicle would soon become an emblem of his remarkable journey through the rugged terrains and unexpected turns that lay ahead in Somalia.

We then briefly returned to the UK, where Dad effectively went back to school to learn new skills for his forthcoming posting. His career to date in the Foreign Office had been as a Communications Officer for the Diplomatic Wireless Service (DWS), and now he had been promoted to the Cultural Attaché and the Head of the British Council, his role would, needless to say, significantly change. Indeed, he would still have communications responsibility for the mission as well as a number of other confidential tasks. His role was to sell Britain and to build cultural relations at a key tipping point in Somalia's history between the then Communist East and the Capitalist West.

On one of our first evenings, we did pay a visit to the Liido Club just along the hotel. The Liido Club was a long-standing haunt of ex-pats. Essentially it was a bar facing out to sea. One notable resident of the Liido Club was a rather aggressive baboon. Clearly, this animal had been tormented by local children and used to chase off any local that approached the bar. Said baboon took a dislike to my brother and chased him, then aged 5 across the beach and then bit him on the back of the leg. Mum went absolutely berserk! At which point we immediately left. Regrettably, the bar was marred by a glaring and disheartening presence of racism and hostility towards Somalis. It was an atmosphere where intolerance prevailed, and Somalis were made to feel unwelcome and subjected to offensive and racist remarks when daring to approach the establishment. This overt display of discrimination left no doubt that this was not a place meant for us. Coupled with the distressing incident involving the baboon, our brief encounter with the Liido Club cast a lasting shadow over our entire two-year stay in Somalia. While it is possible that others may hold cherished memories of the club, for us, it epitomised the grim reality of white racism and misogyny that we encountered far too often on our travels.

I should also point out that at that time that as beautiful as the vista of the Liido was, swimming in the sea was impossible. The sea was infested with Zambezi River sharks and reef sharks on account of the abattoir built at the north end of the bay. Indeed, during our time in Mogadishu, children were sadly taken in less than a foot of water and died pretty instantly on the beach. The abattoir dumped its waste directly into the sea, and sharks having an immensely efficient sense of smell, could pick up the abattoir waste from hundreds of miles away down the East African coast and would converge on the waters off the coast of Mogadishu. We heard terrible stories of our distraught doctor trying to desperately save the lives of children on the beach who had inadvertently gone into the water to retrieve a ball only to be taken by sharks. Despite vain attempts to save lives, our doctor was repeatedly met with disappointment.

That particular week proved to be an arduous test for our family, and the stay at Al Uruba Hotel, coupled with other challenging circumstances, took a toll on my poor Dad's emotional well-being, resulting in him breaking down only the second day. However, as fate would have it, the departure of the Westcombes signalled a turning point for us. We bid farewell to the hotel and embraced a fresh start as we settled into our comparatively luxurious embassy-provided villa. The memories of Al Uruba quickly faded into the distance, becoming a mere footnote in our journey. Throughout the remainder of our time in Mogadishu, we avoided setting foot inside that hotel, and we refrained from recommending it to any visiting guests. Simultaneously, just as a new chapter began, my Dad's eagerly awaited Land Rover, shipped via sea freight from Jeddah, finally arrived, granting us the freedom and convenience of having our own wheels to explore our new home of Mogadishu and the surrounding area. With the Land Rover at our disposal, a renewed sense of independence and possibility greeted us.

Jazeerah south of Mogadishu

Prized Somali camels

Chapter 2 – A Land of Breathtaking Beauty

As you traverse the breathtakingly beautiful Somali landscape, you find yourself immersed in a mesmerising and alluring tapestry of a rugged and untamed wilderness. The vast expanse stretches before you, revealing an arid and desolate land that simultaneously enthrals and challenges. The beauty lies in its unforgiving nature, a stark contrast of nature's power and the resilience of life that manages to thrive against all odds.

The first thing that strikes you is the sheer vastness of the Somali landscape. It stretches as far as the eye can see, extending to all directions endlessly, a sprawling canvas of untouched earth and boundless sky. The terrain is dominated by barren and rocky plains devoid of lush vegetation aside from the scrub bushes and the occasional acacia tree. The ground itself is sun-baked and dusty, painted in earthy tones that reflect the relentless sun overhead. With each step, the fine particles of sand make way beneath your feet, carried by the persistent winds that whisper solitude and remoteness.

Yet, amidst the harshness and austerity of the environment, there exists an undeniable beauty that permeates the Somali landscape. The golden rays and hues of the sun cast a warm and ethereal glow upon the surroundings, infusing the scene with a touch of otherworldly charm. At sunrise and sunset shadows stretch across the rugged terrain, creating a captivating interplay of light and darkness that enchants the observer. It is a sight that takes your breath away as the contrasting colours and textures harmoniously coalesce into a visual feast for the senses. At midday and the sun's zenith it is scorching hot and there is nowhere to hide from the intense heat.

Within ten metres of leaving the tarmac you are immediately isolated and alone and you feel almost lost. It is very hard to orientate yourself without the sun. Everything looks the same. Like mirages emerging from the arid expanse, large clumps of scrub bush appear, offering a momentary brief respite from the unforgiving aridity. These meagre patches of greenery are an essential source of nourishment to the nomad's cattle and their existence a testament to nature's ingenuity to be present in such a harsh environment and demonstrate a delicate balance between survival and adaptation.

The landscape's primal charm lies in its untouched and untamed state and has done so for many thousands of years. In this captivating place, the modern world seems distant, and time seems to stand still. Ancient rock formations rise majestically, bearing witness to centuries of geological transformation. The sheer magnitude of these structures is awe-inspiring, and their weathered surfaces reveal the stories of countless years.

Despite the absence of towering trees, the Somali landscape possesses its own unique allure. Low-lying shrubs and resilient vegetation cling tenaciously to the rocky outcrops, their vibrant colours offering a stark contrast against the backdrop of the barren sandy earth. These pockets of life become sanctuaries for a diverse array of wildlife, from nimble gazelle, or dik-dik, gracefully leaping across the plains to a myriad of bird species, including vultures and ospreys, soaring through the expansive cloudless blue sky.

The landscape's remoteness feels like an undiscovered frontier, a place waiting to be explored and understood. In the Somali landscape, one finds solace in the tranquillity that permeates the air. The absence of human habitation accentuates the silence, broken only by the whispers of the wind. It is a place where one can truly appreciate the raw power and resilience of nature, where the elements shape the land and leave an indelible mark on the soul of anyone who ventures here.

The Somali landscape is a land of contrasts and contradictions. In the hinterland the scrub bush is barren, desiccated, dry, devoid of moisture, devoid of life, isolated, and soulless. On the coast you are rewarded with the mesmerising soft white pearlescent sand, the small coves, the beautiful semi-circular pristine beaches and turquoise sea. And yet around Afgooye and the Shebelle River you are able to relax and take refuge in the fertile, lush green shade, and the cool shadow of tall trees.

The rugged terrain and expansive vistas create a sense of vastness, igniting the imagination and evoking a sense of isolation and remoteness. Every step carries you further into the heart of the land, unravelling its mysteries and revealing its hidden wonders. You feel cut off from the world. Alone. It is as though you are literally on another planet.

Traditionally, Somalis living outside of towns and cities have embraced a nomadic or semi-nomadic way of life intricately tied to the vastness and challenges of the Somali landscape. They have been resilient stewards of the land, adapting to its arid conditions and utilising its resources to sustain themselves and their communities. In the early 1980s more than 75% of the Somali population of roughly 8 million people was nomadic or semi-nomadic, less than 2 million people were living in towns and cities and between 4 and 5 hundred thousand people lived in Mogadishu.

Nomadic pastoralism has been the cornerstone of Somali life for centuries, shaping their cultural identity and forging a deep connection with the land they call home. Families, organized into clans, would embark on cyclical migrations with their herds of camels, sheep, and goats in search of water and grazing lands, guided by the timeless wisdom passed down through generations. These nomadic clans formed the backbone of Somali society, and their ability to adapt and thrive in the face of the land's challenges was evidence of their resilience.

The nomadic lifestyle was intricately woven into the fabric of Somali society. The Somali people's traditional livelihood revolved around their herds. They would rely on camel milk, meat, and hides for sustenance and trade, while sheep and goats provided wool, meat, and milk. The nomadic lifestyle fostered a symbiotic relationship between the people and their animals, with the nomads respecting and caring for their herds as integral members of their families. As the nomads traversed the challenging Somali landscape, they formed a profound bond with their surroundings. They relied on their deep knowledge of the land, honed over generations, to navigate its intricacies. Their mobility was essential, enabling them to adapt to the ever-changing conditions and ensuring their livestock's survival.

The traditional Somali dwelling, known as an "*aqal*," was a portable and practical structure perfectly suited for a nomadic lifestyle. Crafted from a framework of wooden poles, branches, and woven mats, skilfully intertwined and secured, the aqal was a dome-shaped hut. Its design allowed for easy dismantling and transport to a new location as the nomadic clans migrated across the vast Somali landscape. The aqal's walls were created by weaving together mats made from durable natural fibres, offering shelter from the scorching sun. The interplay of light and shadow cast by the woven walls created an intimate and comforting ambience within, offering a sense of home and security amidst the ever-changing expanse of nomadic life.

The nomadic lifestyle fostered a strong sense of community and mutual support among Somalis. Extended families, bound by blood and shared heritage, would often travel together, forming temporary camps known as *"daanto"* or *"gurti."* These camps would become lively social hubs where people of all ages gathered to share stories, songs, and traditional dances. The rhythmic beats of the famous *"daanto"*, accompanied by hand claps and foot-stomping, reverberate through the air, energizing the atmosphere with a sense of vitality and celebration. Meanwhile, the melodic verses of the *"buraanbur"*, sung in melodic unison, carried the tales of the nomadic life, evoking a deep connection with their ancestral roots. These vibrant gatherings provided a way for the nomads to preserve their cultural heritage and maintain a sense of belonging amidst their transient existence.

In the Somali landscape, water was a scarce and precious resource, and its acquisition required ingenuity and cooperation. Traditional wells, known as *"berkads"*, were meticulously dug to access hidden groundwater reserves. These wells, carefully lined and maintained, became lifelines in the arid terrain, providing a vital source of water for the nomads and their herds. Meanwhile, the nomads would strategically identify natural depressions and seasonal riverbeds that would serve as temporary water sources during the rainy season.

Water was carefully conserved, and the knowledge of locating and managing water sources was passed down through generations, ensuring the nomads' survival in the harsh environment. They represented the essence of Somali cultural heritage, embodying resourcefulness, adaptability, and a deep connection with the land. In the face of the ever-changing Somali landscape, these traditions served as pillars of strength, ensuring the nomads' physical well-being and sustaining their rich sense of identity and community.

Trade played a vital role in the nomadic Somali way of life. Caravans, known as *"doolo"*, embarked on arduous journeys, traversing vast distances and connecting different clans and regions. These bustling caravans served as lifelines of economic independence, facilitating the exchange of goods, such as livestock, textiles, and spices, that sustained the nomadic communities. Laden with diverse treasures, the caravans brought together the nomads' prized possessions, such as livestock, renowned for their strength and adaptability to the harsh environment, as well as intricately woven textiles displaying vibrant colours and traditional patterns. These caravans established trade routes, linking the interior of the country with coastal towns and cities, creating a vibrant tapestry of commerce that fuelled the nomadic lifestyle and fostered social and economic cohesion.

The nomadic Somali way of life was not without challenges. The harsh and unpredictable nature of the environment presented constant threats to the nomads' existence. Droughts, with their relentless grasp, could transform the landscape into a parched and barren expanse, pushing the nomads to the limits of their resourcefulness. Locust invasions, like swarms of voracious invaders, threatened the nomads' precious vegetation and grazing lands, testing their resilience in the face of natural calamities. Moreover, conflicts over limited resources, such as water and grazing rights, posed ongoing challenges, demanding delicate negotiations and peaceful resolutions to maintain the fragile balance of nomadic coexistence. However, their unwavering resilience and adaptability allowed them to weather these hardships and continue their ancestral traditions.

While urbanisation and modernization have brought changes to Somali society, the nomadic way of life continues to hold deep cultural significance. It serves as a testament to the Somali people's enduring connection with their land, their reliance on community and cooperation, and their ability to thrive amidst adversity. The traditions and values shaped by generations of nomadic living continue to shape the identity and resilience of the Somali people today, reflecting their rich heritage and the unwavering spirit that has sustained them throughout history.

As the Somali people navigate the complexities of a changing world, the lessons learned from their nomadic ancestors remain a source of inspiration and guidance. The nomadic way of life symbolizes the strength and adaptability of the Somali people, reminding them of the inherent wisdom embedded in their cultural heritage.

Needless to say, camels play an important role in Somali life. Quite often, outside the walls of our house on Afgooye Road, we would hear the sound of commotion: the sound of animals and people shouting and whistling. We would rush to the open gate to see and hear large herds of camels, or *geel*, being moved down the road to the city market to be sold or, indeed, directly to the port to be shipped to Saudi Arabia or the Gulf.

In the pastoral lifestyle of Somalia, camels play a myriad of significant roles, with milk production being perhaps the most crucial. Camel meat is a sought-after delicacy, especially during festive occasions. Moreover, male camels serve as a means of transportation, carrying water and household items when families migrate to new grazing lands.

To quote a Somali proverb, "*If the camel is fine, our life is fine*". The traditional social fabric of Somali society also places camels at its core; they are used in the dowry system and in settling disputes within clan feuds. Larger herd size is often seen as a status symbol, reflecting social standing within the community. In the context of the Somali traditional economy, camels act as a primary reserve, providing a safety net against drought, disease, and other natural disasters, or at least they did forty years ago.

Somalia, unique as the birthplace of camel domestication, boasts the highest camel population worldwide. Unlike other global regions where farming prevails, Somalis prior to the Civil War, typically led a nomadic lifestyle.

Camels are venerated as invaluable beasts of burden, providing sustenance and purpose to the nomad. Camel milk in Somalia is as vital as cow's milk in the West, with few Somalis consuming the latter. It is believed that Somalia's name derives from the phrase "*soo maal*", meaning "go milk (the camel)." This phrase is frequently used when addressing guests, underlining the significance of both hospitality and camel milk in Somali culture.

During the rainy season, *geelxir*, or herders, minding camel flocks, might consume as much as ten litres of milk daily. The geelxir are young unmarried men who manage the herd and live separately from the clan. They have no fixed abode and literally stop and camp wherever the herd grazes at the end of the day.

Elderly camels may be culled for their flesh, particularly when visitors are anticipated for a festive occasion, and the fatty hump of the camel is esteemed as a gourmet treat.

A few years after leaving Somalia, I visited Imbaba Camel Market to the north west of Cairo in Egypt, where you would historically find Somali camels and may still do today, although the conflict in Sudan may have hampered their transit. The Imbaba camel market (Souk El Gamal) has now moved to Birqash camel market also to the north west of Cairo.

They are by far the most regal and the most expensive camels. Their keepers would show deference and respect for this prized commodity and, unlike other breeds, refrain from pushing them around, and by extension, they are generally less agitated than their non-Somali counterparts. The Somali camel is, on average, about 3 metres in height with beautiful dark brown eyes. They are also one-humped or dromedary.

Forty years ago, Somali camels were transported by truck or by foot all the way from Somalia to Imbaba in Egypt, a distance of roughly 2,000 miles, and were fed the very best grass and grains on their transit. Today camels are moved by sea to Egypt through the Red Sea ports of either Safaga or Ein Soukna, but historically, they would have been moved overland through Eritrea to Sudan and then on to Egypt on what is known as the *Darb El Arba'in* or the infamous Forty Days Road.

The name comes from the number of days the journey would take in antiquity, but it was a key route on the Trans-Saharan trade routes. Trade goods and livestock would be moved on the *Darb El Arba'in* through a chain of oases as they have done for thousands of years.

To understand the importance of camels, in part, is to know Somalia.

***

As a footnote, to understand just how much camels are venerated in Somalia I read a few years ago about the following news story: In January 2020 in South Australia during an extremely intense hot drought, camels were being shot by snipers from the air. Whilst the action was humane, it was met with outrage thousands of miles away in Somalia with calls for the camels to be "repatriated" back to Somalia. Camels were introduced into Australia in the early to mid-19th century as a key form of transport. Known as "Gans", a derivative of 'Afghanistan' given many were introduced from Afghanistan and what is now Pakistan and India by the British. But it is thought that some camels were also shipped to Australia from what was British Somaliland, hence the cries from Somalia for repatriation. Memories are long in Somalia and nobody forgets.

An Aqal

Nomad carrying water on camel

Woman gathering firewood

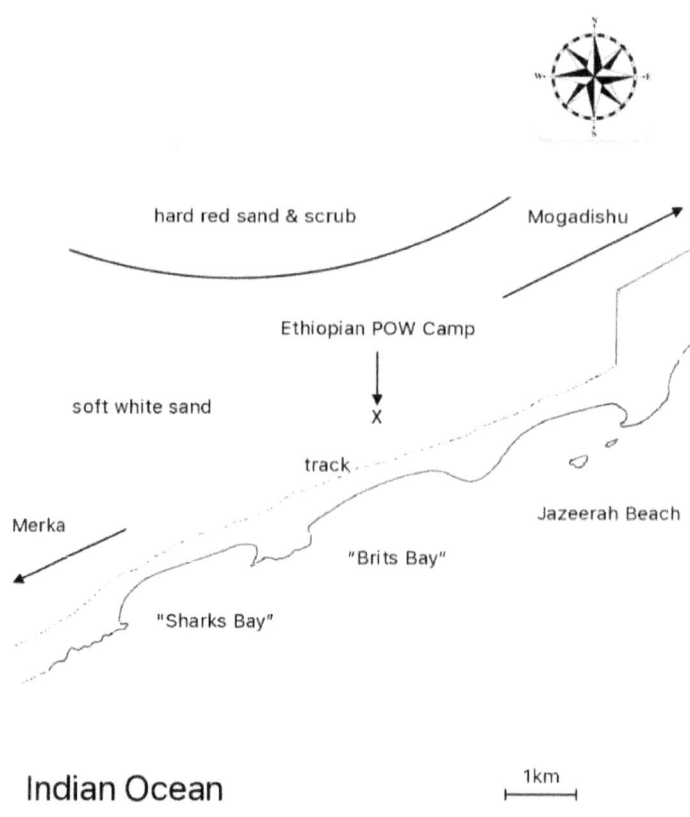

Frequented Beaches

Chapter 3 – Sunny Days by the Sea

Most people in Europe or North America, on reading or hearing the word "Somalia", would naturally associate it with war, terrorism, starvation, famine, and death because, fundamentally, anyone's perception of the country and its people is completely consumed by what people see or read in the media. It is entirely to be expected and isn't necessarily pejorative but rather just a visualisation of Somalia as seen through the lens of the ever-common media reports. However, behind the veil of these perceptions lies a different reality, one that remains largely hidden from the world.

Similarly, in my experience, if you said to someone that Somalia boasts some of the most beautiful beaches in the world and an abundance of marine life, they would look at you with disbelief and possibly madness, and again this is entirely to be expected given most people's reference. However, my recollections of Somalia's beaches from some forty years ago give me confidence that they are, for the most part, as beautiful today as they were then. These beaches of Somalia, with their pristine stretches of powdery sand and crystal-clear turquoise waters, indeed rival those found in renowned destinations like Seychelles and the Maldives and are arguably the most beautiful in the Indian Ocean. Along the Somali coastline, nature unveils its breath-taking geography, where brilliant white pearlescent sand fringed shores meet the gently lapping waves of the Indian Ocean. The vibrant marine life that inhabits the coastal waters adds to the allure, with colourful coral reefs teeming with a kaleidoscope of fish and other aquatic creatures.

Yet, it is undeniable that the beauty and splendour of Somalia's beaches and marine life often go unnoticed. The focus on the country's challenges and the overshadowing veil of terror and brutal jihadism have muted the recognition of this natural wonder. But I acknowledge it is hard to see behind the veil of terror and brutal jihadism. The world's perception of Somalia has been shaped predominantly by stories of conflict and struggle, making it difficult for the true beauty of the land to shine through.

However, behind the tumultuous headlines, there is a Somalia that remains resilient, holding on to its inherent natural treasures. That said, for many years now, I have held the sincere view that its natural beauty could be a pathway to national prosperity. Not in terms of exploitation of its natural resources, to which there are many reports of its coastal waters fisheries being plundered by unregulated and illegal fishing, but in terms of people choosing to visit Somalia and holiday as they would to other Indian Ocean resorts such as in the Maldives or Seychelles. It is a land of stunning landscapes, where in the north of the Horn, rugged mountains carve their way through the horizons, and fertile plains embrace the cycle of life. It is a place where ancient ruins whisper tales of rich history, and traditional nomadic communities continue to thrive amidst the vastness of the Somali wilderness.

Somalia's beauty, both in its natural wonders and cultural heritage, is diverse and breath-taking and serves as a reminder that there is more to the country than what meets the eye. As the plane begins its descent just north of Kismayo on approach to Mogadishu, the captivating view unfolds before your eyes. From the window, mile after mile of pristine, glistening white sandy beaches stretch along the coast. The view is nothing short of breath-taking, evoking a strong desire, and you just want to be there, to feel the soft sand between your toes, and to slip into its cool waters abundant with marine life.

However, the beauty of the coastal expanse is tinged with sadness as you realize that today much of the territory from around Merka south to Kismayo is under the control of Al Shabaab. This reality casts a shadow over the pristine beaches, limiting access to these stunning landscapes and inhibiting the full enjoyment and appreciation of their splendour.

Given our disappointment with the Liido Club, we were determined never to return and rather find somewhere we could relax. The first place we were introduced to was the Jazeerah Beach. Situated along the coast road past the airport and the Saddam Hussein-funded refinery ended and so was accessible to two-wheel drive vehicles.

I can't remember exactly who introduced us to Jazeerah Beach, but I vaguely recall a visit with the then-British Ambassador, Michael Purcell and his wife at the very start of our sojourn in Somalia. It was one of the rare outings they actually made to the beach with us as they preferred the seclusion of their Italian colonial-styled residence on a slight hill overlooking the city rather than the foray to the beach. With a private swimming pool solely for their use, the allure of venturing to the beach probably seemed like an unnecessary hassle and who could blame them.

Whilst we did have access to a pool at the American Embassy Compound, going to the beach was an opportunity to get away from the heat of Mogadishu and bathe in the cool waters of the bay at Jazeerah. It was an opportunity to get away, relax and have some fun.

The rhythmic sound of the waves crashing against the shore provided a soothing backdrop, harmonizing with the gentle rustle of the palm fronds swaying in the coastal breeze. The beach's untouched beauty extended as far as the eye could see, inviting visitors to stroll along its expansive shores, leaving footprints in the fine sand. I should point out at this point that while sharks were still a problem at Jazeerah Beach, the presence of a perfectly intact reef acted as a natural barrier, reducing the risk. However, still a possibility of a 6-foot reef shark cruising into the bay and getting stranded as the tide receded. Despite this, there were remarkably few incidents of shark attacks reported at Jazeerah Beach, a significant contrast to the thirty or so fatalities that occurred on Liido Beach between 1977 and 1987.

To reach Jazeerah Beach, we embarked on a relatively short drive from Mogadishu. Passing by the airport and then the oil refinery, the transition from the tarmac to a dirt road marked the beginning of our journey south. As we continued on the road, the landscape gradually transformed, revealing a diverse tapestry of coastal scenery. The bumpy motion of the vehicle along the dusty and potholed path created a sense of anticipation, a prelude to the serenity and natural beauty that awaited us. Arriving at Jazeerah Beach, we parked our vehicle just south of the headland, strategically positioning ourselves to overlook the vast expanse of the sea. In preparation for the sun's intense midday rays, we secured a tarpaulin along the side of my Dad's long-wheelbase V8 Land Rover. This improvised shelter provided respite from the scorching heat, casting a welcome shade under which we sought refuge. The panoramic view stretched as far as the eye could see, capturing the infinite horizon where the sky met the ocean. The rhythmic ebb and flow of the waves echoed a timeless symphony, soothing our senses and inviting us to immerse ourselves in the coastal retreat. Seashells, delicately scattered along the beach, whispered stories of marine life's treasures washed ashore, inviting us to collect them as souvenirs of our coastal escapade. The sand was a brilliant white, and the beach arched between two headlands to form a large bay. The bay was importantly protected with a visible reef at low tide. That was important given the high prevalence of sharks in the area. In other words, the reef helped keep the sharks out of what was relatively shallow swimming water. We would also initially take the precaution of scouting for sharks before swimming.

The constant rhythm of the waves provided a soothing soundtrack, creating a symphony of nature that transported us to a state of calm and relaxation — in this serene coastal haven, time seemed to slow down. At Jazeerah Beach, we revelled in the simplicity of the moment, cherishing the feeling of warm sand between our toes and the refreshing sea breeze caressing our faces.

Standing on the headland, in solitude, looking out to the vast expanse of the sea, there was no other mark of human existence, and an eerie silence enveloped the landscape. Today, looking at the same area in Google Maps, you will see an abundance of homes and businesses now built on top of the headland as though they had always been there, erasing the traces of its natural beauty. I am sure at the height of the Civil War in Mogadishu, many families escaped the city for the safety of Jazeerah and made their homes there. Again, all entirely understandable, given the horrors of what unfolded in the city.

Jazeerah Beach was defined by a protruding rocky sandstone headland that overlooked it, which had sharp jagged coral rocks that jutted out into the sea. From the headland, you extended over the reef and could see the deep waters below. Due to wave erosion, the headland protruded out over the sea, offering a unique vantage point to observe the intricate reef below. The headland effectively marked one end of the reef extending across the beach to the next headland. Looking out to sea, you had safe beaches on either side. I say safe because "safety" was granted on account of the reef.

In other words, the larger predatory animals were pend out of the shallower water by the projecting barrier of the reef.

Within sight, directly in front of our favourite spot and just to the right of the northerly headland, was a small island. Perched atop the island was an old grave, serving as a sacred shrine to a Sufi Imam. While the island itself wasn't easily accessible, we occasionally visited it by dingy and walked around the island looking back to our camp on the beach.

Just to the northwest of the headland were salt flats that were still very much in production in the early 1980s. These salt flats, encompassed by a series of locks and channels, controlled the flow of seawater into the settling pans. Through the process of evaporation, the salt would be gradually collected and shovelled into wooden wheelbarrows. Then on a flat raised area adjacent to the settling pans, the salt would be piled into perfectly formed pyramidal mounds to dry out further before being shipped off. The salt pans held salt water of different concentrations, the most concentrated being salt itself. The settling pans themselves exhibited a brilliant pink hue, adding a touch of vibrant colour to the coastal scenery. The salt itself was raw and not particularly edible or appetising to sight.

I recall diving around the lock where at low tide and in the mid-afternoon, the overhanging rock cast a long shadow. The locked gates were made of wood, and by the looks of them, they were old and well-used but remarkably effective. As I ventured into the cool water, the tranquillity and freshness enveloped me, and I marvelled at the abundance of life that flourished in this hidden underwater realm. Around the lock gates was an abundance of catfish and small crayfish hiding in the shade the rocks and lock gates provided. Interestingly, I seldom encountered catfish anywhere else. Spotting catfish resting gently in the shade, I endeavoured to catch one with my bare hands, only to be disappointed!

The Jazeerah Beach served as an idyllic setting for relaxation and unwinding. My Mum would prepare tuna sandwiches for our beach outings. We would pick up long bread rolls fresh from the bakery en route, and Mum would cut them open and then scrape out the doughy part of the roll in the middle, which was always full of weevils, small black ant-sized animals that we always discovered without fail in our bread. The sandwich filling was always the same - tinned tuna! And given local food scarcity, there wasn't a great deal of alternatives.

In the pristine waters of the bay, we would bathe, play, snorkel and spearfish. Dad had a compressed gas speargun, and I used a far more rudimentary one powered with rubber bands. The sea was abundant with fish of various species, including tuna, red snapper, scorpion fish, and puffer fish. On occasion, he would inadvertently and accidentally spear a puffer fish which would immediately inflate and effectively bring an end to our fishing expedition! Again, it was entirely unintentional and everything we caught we ate but spearing a puffer fish subsequently created a hazard and removing the dead fish from the spear was an absolute nightmare on account of its rubbery and impenetrable skin and the sharpness of its spikes.

On the other hand, if we caught a red snapper, there was much jubilation. Partly because of harpooning a meaty fish, but more importantly, there is nothing more delicious than a grilled red snapper on the barbecue! Dad would clean up the fish at the beach, removing the scales and its guts and then place the fish in the cool box to be barbecued later at home.

Fish was a significant part of our diet in Somalia. There was one fisherman who we would religiously buy his fish from. Close to Jazeerah and literally out of the middle of nowhere, a fisherman would appear. Despite the fisherman's disability — a missing hand resulting from a shark attack — he remained a friendly and resilient individual, always offering a remarkable assortment of fish. He would carry the fish in a large sack over his shoulder and then would carefully take the fish out of the sack and set them out on the sand. Among his various catches would be red snapper, mackerel, large tuna and, importantly, enormous lobsters. My Dad would eagerly purchase a variety of fish from him, appreciating the flavours and freshness they brought to our meals.

The preparation of the tuna differed from the other catches. It would be chopped up into large pieces and then boiled up on the stove, with the heads and tails. Once cooled, the tuna pieces were placed in plastic containers and frozen for later use. It wasn't a particularly pleasant smell, but our dog, Brandy, absolutely devoured the tuna. Unusually perhaps the dog loved fish which is why it had been called "Skippy" (after skipjack tuna) by a prior owner.

As regards the lobster, this was naturally prized. My Mum would pick out large Indian Ocean lobster, gigantic compared to the tiddlers on sale in Padstow. Indian Ocean lobster, *Panulirus Versicolor*, have no claws but two spiny rostra over their eyes and two large antennae. These are quite the sight. These were usually served by Mum as a lobster Thermidor over fragrant steamed rice. The lobster was always very meaty and went down a treat with dinner guests, particularly those visiting from the UK. Whilst I wasn't a fan of fish per se at that age, I have to say this dish was delicious.

Looking back now and reflecting on those precious memories, we perhaps took for granted the freshness of the fish that was available to us.

What is interesting is that for a country with an abundance of marine life along the Somali coast, Somalis then and now do not commonly consume fish and their preference is for kid goat, camel or beef. Somalis are essentially pastoralists, and there has always been a taboo on the consumption of fish, chicken and eggs. Some Somalis have suggested that they simply don't like the smell of fish.

The immutable statistic is that less than 1% of Somalis eat fish. There is and remains a huge distrust for anything that comes from the sea and consumption of fish by the general population remains very low. Whilst it is perhaps easy to judge a country which has endured such famine and food poverty, the mistrust is ingrained in the Somali psyche spanning back many hundreds of years, if not thousands. Whilst parallels can be unhelpful, it does remind me to a degree of the long-time distrust that exists between farmers and fishermen in Cornwall and how that over time has taken an often-nonsensical life of its own.

With over 3,000 kilometres of coastline fishing was identified as a sector with enormous potential and in the early 1980s special attention was directed towards fishing following the terrible famine of the mid-1970s. Fish was seen as an immediate source of food for a growing population. Indeed, my Dad worked in a project to bring fishing skills to Somalia through the ODA in partnership with other European countries including Sweden and Denmark. Whilst data shows a marked improvement at the end of the 1980s verses the beginning, with some 18,000 tonnes of fish being caught at the end of the 1980s, one factor remained: Fish continue to be treated with suspicion by the essentially pastoralist population and fishing remained a largely unexploited sector, contributing less than 1 percent of GDP in 1990!

For us fish was also difficult to come by with us only really being able to purchase either from the solitary fisherman at the Jazeerah Beach or from one of the only stalls selling it at the entrance to the Bakaara market.

Sadly, in recent years, the waters off the Somali coast have fallen victim to illegal fishing activities perpetuated by both Somali pirates and foreign fishing fleets, including those from China. The exponential increase in illegal fishing has become a significant international problem, depleting Somali fish stocks and disrupting the delicate marine ecosystem. While efforts have been made by the Federal Government of Somalia to require fishing boats to report their catch, effective policing remains an ongoing challenge.

The coastal waters of the sea were a vibrant ecosystem, teeming with a variety of fish, including large tuna, grouper, red snapper, scorpion or lionfish, pipe fish and lobster, as well as a whole host of others. Along the shore ran small inedible crabs, adding a touch of liveliness to the coastal scenery.

We did try and venture to a neighbouring bay that inadvertently was right next door to an Ethiopian prisoner of war camp. Contrary to the conventional image of a POW camp, the camp wasn't much of a camp and not what you would associate with preconceived ideas of what a POW camp should be. The prisoners were dressed in white shorts, tunics and hats and no shoes, their bare feet exposed to the rugged terrain. Their attire, though simplistic, served as a constant reminder of their captive status. In other words, they were highly visible, and any escape would be futile. The camp's location left little room for escape or anonymity. The 200 kilometres walk through unforgiving terrain to the border would have posed insurmountable challenges for any prisoner attempting to flee undetected. Moreover, crossing the treacherous expanse of the Ogaden, devoid of water, supplies, and a change of clothing, would have rendered escape all but impossible. So, needless to say, they didn't go anywhere and depended entirely on the hospitality of their Somali hosts, resigned to their captive existence.

On one occasion, I inadvertently ventured into said confines of the camp....

So called "Brits Bay"

Chapter 4 - Walking into a POW camp

How does one inadvertently wander into a prisoner of war camp? First of all, this is Africa - affectionately referenced by the three-letter acronym 'T.I.A.' - and in Africa, anything extraordinary is possible! As mentioned, this prisoner-of-war camp was to hold specifically Ethiopian conscripts from the Ogaden War. Just by way of background, the Ogaden War, also known as the Ethio-Somali War (*Dagaalkii Xoraynta Soomaali Galbeed* in Somali), was a military conflict between Somalia and Ethiopia from July 1977 to March 1978 over the contested region of the Ogaden. Somalia invaded in 1977, much to the disapproval of the Soviet Union, given the Ethiopian regime under Mengistu Halai Mariam, was fast becoming a Marxist-Leninist state despite two years of the Ethiopian Civil War from 1975 to 1977. Mengistu, backed by Soviet advisors, led by General Vasily Petrov, and military hardware and personnel from Cuba courtesy of Fidel Castro, buoyed on from winning his first African conflict in Angola, fought off the Somali National Army (SNA). Many conscripts were picked up and transported to these makeshift camps, where they effectively languished. You will note the context that the war ended in 1978, and yet Somalia held POWs until the early 1980s. Arguably this conflict was another factor that contributed to Somalia's subsequent Civil War some fifteen years later due to heavy disapproval from the population and a demoralised and disorganised SNA.

So, how did I inadvertently wander into the camp? Quite simply, it was a mere consequence of a seemingly innocent outing. The family, seeking some recreational activity, decided to spend another weekend at the beach. My friend Brian and I went off with our spears hunting dik-dik or small gazelle. We were not paying attention at all to where we were going and were just wandering aimlessly around the scrubland behind our beach camp. As I said, there was no formal perimeter fence and no lookout guards. To our surprise, we found ourselves amidst a group of men dressed in thick white cotton shorts, shirts, and pointed hats being guarded by the SNA with AK-47 Kalashnikov rifles. A few of the prisoners spoke English and acted as translators between us and the guards, who, by this time, had detained us. They wanted to know what we were doing and why we were near them. Naively we explained that we were just hunting with spears and looking for dik-dik. They were intrigued, and perhaps on reflection, we were the only white people they had seen for a very long time. The prisoners didn't look particularly bothered or undernourished and seemed quite happy to be held captive. They were being used by the SNA to help pan for salt in the salt flats just to the north of Jazeerah Beach.

Eventually, one of the guards said he would let me go but kept Brian and asked that I return with my Dad. I quickly left the camp and headed back towards the beach to find my parents. I was breathless when I caught up with him, and then the realisation dawned on me that what we had done was perhaps not safe at all. I explained to my Dad what had happened. I could see that he was very stressed. He got up and followed me up the hill away from the beach across the scrub towards the camp. Running towards us, heading back to the beach, was Brian shouting, "Turn around! Turn around!" Heeding his plea, we did just that and changed our direction. Needless to say, we never went wandering again and were naturally briefly reprimanded.

Fast forward five years, I was at school in England, and during my time there, we were encouraged to write a personal short story as part of a creative writing exercise supported by our local newspaper, the Banbury Guardian. The intent was to introduce us to different styles of writing as part of our A-Level General Studies course. In this case, it was journalism and writing for newspapers.

Taking inspiration from my experience, I duly wrote a short story about the prisoner of war camp. Needless to say, part of the intent was to make the story attention-grabbing and interesting to the reader! Little did I anticipate the consequences that awaited. Soon after submitting my short story homework to the newspaper and a few days later, I was asked for an interview. Naively assuming it was merely a follow-up to the writing exercise, I obliged without much thought. What followed was a full-blown interview. Thinking nothing further of it, a week or so passed and then, to my surprise, my story was plastered all over the front page of the newspaper with a headline that read, "Prisoners in a Somali desert camp!" Under the headline was my story re-written and quotes from me extracted from my short story!

Prisoners in a Somali desert camp

BY JESS CARTER

Looking down the barrel of a Kalashnikov gun and being marched to a Somalian prisoner of war camp is something Bloxham school pupil Stephen Tunnicliffe will never forget.

The son of a British diplomat working for the foreign office, Stephen, 17, has spent most of his life globe-trotting, and living in countries such as Ethiopia, Somalia, Egypt, Australia and Saudi Arabia.

He has encountered many things along the way, and said: "I've been spoilt, I have seen quite a lot and I have experienced a striking contrast between living well and hardship, hardship more often."

He has never forgotten the day he and a friend strayed from the beach where their parents were, into an Ethiopian prisoner-of-war camp, which had no barbed-wire or defences surrounding it, because the Ethiopian border was 500 miles away over a hot desert.

SURPRISE

Stephen, who was then 11-years-old, and his friend, were hunting small birds with home-made catapults over the sand dunes, until they reached a flat plain.

"To my surprise both my friend and I were looking down the end of a Kalashnikov machin gun. I think it was then that I thought I was going to die," said Stephen.

"The soldier, to me, looked a giant. He was wearing olive-green army dress, and dusty boots, his beret was traded for an arab headdress. His black face shone in the light, and when he smiled his teeth were a striking contrast, brilliant white," remembers Stephen.

"We didn't understand what he was saying but followed the directions given by the gun."

Stephen says the Somalians didn't treat their prisoners of war by the Geneva Convention. The boys were taken to the cells, which Stephen remembers as being "like a sauna", and given bananas to eat, the staple diet of the prisoners, some of whom had been in the camp for years.

"The Geneva Convention stipulates that prisoners of war should have at least one meal a day, if necessary be seen by a doctor, and have good sanitary facilities.

"This is where the camp fell down, I didn't touch the drinking water because it was more likely to be infected than the bananas. For a toilet, they had an iron box in the corner of the room, during the day these were filled with petrol and burned. Despite a petrol shortage the army always had enough," he said.

"The Geneva Convention also stipulates that prisoners of war should not be paraded in public where they may face mockery by the enemy. But nevertheless it still went on."

It was only after mentioning the words British Embassy to an Ethiopian prisoner who spoke English, that the situation changed.

"These words led me to freedom. The Ethiopian explained to the guard that my father worked for the British Embassy, he opened the door immediately and let me go, but kept my friend."

HOSTILITY

Stephen said it was Brian's American accent that stopped him leaving the camp. The Somalians felt great hostility towards both the Americans and the Russians, and were not so keen to lose their "enemy" prisoner.

However, when Stephen and his father started back towards the camp, they met Brian running the other way, telling them to turn round.

As he was released, Brian had been told by the soldier, through the Ethiopian translator, not to return, or they might be spending longer there next time.

In the interests of diplomacy, Stephen's father took no action, and Stephen said: "It's one of those things Brian and I will never forget, it was an education. We had seen the conditions a prisoner of war had to suffer. A few hours was enough for me, let alone years."

Banbury Guardian May 1989

The sudden prominence of my tale caught my Dad off guard, and he was rightfully furious. He was very concerned that the front-page story would be subsequently picked up by one of the national newspapers and recirculated. Fortunately, that was as far as it went, but it was a salutary lesson on how something benign could be turned into something much bigger and potentially damaging.

Salt settling pans near the POW camp

Salt mounds next to the salt pans

Chapter 5 - Travelling to Merka

As our time in Somalia unfolded, we travelled to beaches and bays that were much further afield, seeking new experiences and hidden coves. However, the invariable challenge was that Dad was never permitted to be too far away from the embassy, which, given he was the only person technically qualified to operate the communications equipment back in London, was perhaps not surprising. So by extension, other beaches, bays and seaside towns we visited were never more than a few hours' drive away and within radio contact of Dad's colleagues.

A few months further into our tour, we decided to venture further down the alluring coast. There was no proper road but an impassable and arduous sandy way that tested the limits of our vehicle. After passing through deep sand through which my Dad would skilfully manoeuvre in second gear, low range, we reached the precipice of a semi-circular crescent bay that was truly breath-taking and awestriking.

Indeed, this vast expanse of sand was so impossible that we would find other foreigners driving four-wheel drives hopelessly stuck all the way up to the chassis pan of their vehicles. Perversely it became a form of entertainment for us to witness their struggles, observing them futilely attempting to dig themselves out before my father and I would step in to lend a helping hand.

This newfound beach became our sanctuary. A secluded haven of beauty that was also safe to swim in and had also offered tranquillity. We called it "Brits Bay," and indeed, on hearing about it, our friends from other European and the US Embassy would come to this hidden gem.

Increasingly we started moving further south than Jazeerah Beach and began to spend much more time on more secluded and pristine beaches, such as the ironically named Sharks Bay and the ever-enchanting Brits Bay. Again these beaches were not necessarily called as such by Somalis, not named so geographically, but were solely names we gave the beaches we loved and frequented.

We always knew we had found a good beach when the US Marine Corps would turn up. The American Embassy had a detachment of around 30 men providing a security detail at the embassy and the staff accommodation on the Afgooye Road, the so-called "Green Giant" tower block. These off-duty Marines, part of the embassy's security detachment, would arrive on their all-terrain motorbikes and pickups, setting up camp and making the most of their leisure time, where they would barbecue, play American football or just sleep. Their beachfront encampments became coveted spots, as they always seemed to find the prime positions, basking in the idyllic surroundings. We loved these beaches on account of their pristine sand, the crystal-clear waters and also the beautiful, captivating night sky that unfolded its twinkling wonders above us, painting a celestial backdrop for our cherished moments.

On rare occasions, we embarked on a journey to the coastal town of Merka, situated approximately 35 miles south of Jazeerah Beach. Again, whilst it might sound relatively close to Mogadishu, it was quite a journey, as the terrain was challenging. We would head south past the familiar landscapes of Jazeerah Beach, following the sandy track. The sand was incredibly soft in places, and it posed a constant obstacle, and Dad was forever helping pull people stuck in it. So, the going was always slow and would take some time to reach our destination.

The coastline south of Jazeerah Beach to Merka is a breathtaking sight to behold. Picture secluded bays unfurling one after the other along a ribbon of soft white sand that stretches as far as the eye can see. In places like the Maldives or Seychelles, this coastal beauty would be prime real estate, ripe for commercial exploitation. However, here in Somalia, it remains untouched, a pristine meeting point between land and sea.

In the intervening years following the Civil War, Al Shabaab established a foothold in this region, rendering the land extending south from Jazeerah as a treacherous no man's land. Venturing into this territory without armed protection is nothing short of daring.

As you continue your journey southward, the narrow strip of white sand between the shore and the rugged red sand of the hinterland becomes more distinct. The track gradually becomes more passable, granting you an unobstructed view of the captivating coastline ahead. Merka lies on this path, yet only a few vehicles venture this way, as most prefer the longer but quicker route on the tarmac road via Afgooye.

One striking observation is the absence of human habitation, likely due to the scarcity of freshwater. You find yourself truly in the midst of nowhere, immersed in the untamed beauty of the landscape.

Approaching Merka, you find yourself ascending a rise that offers a panoramic view to the south, revealing a small bay cradling the town. Over time, this once reasonably sized settlement has experienced significant growth and sprawl since the early 1980s, transforming into a bustling centre of activity with schools and a hospital.

Merka held a rich historical significance as a port city in the southern Lower Shabelle province of Somalia. It is located approximately 109 km (68 mi) to the southwest of the nation's capital Mogadishu. Merka is the traditional home territory of the Bimal clan and was the centre of the Bimal Revolt or Merka Revolt.

The Port of Merka was the oldest port in Italian Somalia and was affectionately nicknamed the "Port of Bananas" due to its status as a key exporter of bananas from Somalia to Europe. In the city of Merka, there was a huge economic development in the 1930s, due mainly to the growing commerce of the port of Merka connected by a small railway to the farm area of Genale.

On arrival at Merka, we would stay at a guest house where the rooms opened out to the sea. It was extremely basic but safe and a pleasant environment. Memories of the guest house have faded over time, as it lacked any distinctive features or noteworthy experiences. In retrospect, we often found ourselves yearning for the freedom and solitude of camping out on deserted beaches, where we could immerse ourselves in the untamed beauty of the surroundings and forge our own unique experiences.

What I do remember is a small whitewashed high walled courtyard that opened out to the sea. To the back of the courtyard was the accommodation, which was basic and if memory serves me correctly, my parents slept inside with the doors open and I slept outside on a raised searing area in my sleeping bag.

We had a barbecue in the courtyard followed by the mandatory stargazing before bed. What I do recall is the cool breeze from the ocean making sleeping comfortable. There was no air conditioning and there was no fan but neither were needed with a cool breeze straight off the sea.

As the sun set behind us the whitewashed buildings around the bay glowed in the reflected light. It was magical. Merka was special which makes it incredulous and all the harder to subsequently read about it being an Al Shabaab stronghold.

The following morning we rose and had coffee and breakfast before making our way slowly north back to Brits Bay where we would spend the rest of the day before heading home in the evening.

What was the lighthouse in Merka converted to a mosque

Coast heading towards Merka

Pier near Merka

Chapter 6 - Travelling to Warsheikh

Whilst we spent the vast majority of our free time on the beaches to the south of Mogadishu on occasion we did venture north from Mogadishu to Warsheikh. Warsheikh is another small fishing village about 40 miles to the north of Mogadishu along the coast. The journey to Warsheikh was always eventful yet exhilarating. We would have to pass through a Somalia National Army (SNA) tank live firing range. Generally speaking, there wasn't a great deal of activity, and so we witnessed an eerie silence, but on occasion, we would be met by an unexpected tank roaming around in the scrubland through which the track north to Warsheikh passed. There was no way of avoiding it and no alternate routes to select, leaving us in awe and apprehension.

We would generally camp just to the south of Warsheikh on a small, secluded bay with shallow waters to swim in. With each turn, we couldn't help but marvel at the rugged charm of Somalia's untamed wilderness. We would avoid being too close to the town itself primarily out of respect for the local inhabitants, who would have probably frowned on scantily clad foreigners in their swimsuits dipping in and out of the water.

Amongst the many visits to Warsheikh, there came a moment that would forever be etched in our memories - an escapade that could be labelled as both comical and cautionary. Armed with our Somali spears, my friend Brian and I set out on a mission to conquer the shallow waters and capture the elusive fish. Little did we know that our enthusiasm would lead to an unexpected misadventure, and we would end up injuring ourselves.

As we threw our spears like skilled hunters, we soon realized that catching fish was an art mastered by patience and precision, not wild thrusts. We also learnt the dangers of running with sharp spears. In our eagerness to prove ourselves, fate intervened, and calamity struck. I stabbed myself in the back of the leg with my three-pronged spear, meant for the fishes, and my poor friend Brian slipped and sliced the palm of his hand open between the thumb and the palm. The blade was so sharp that the spear cut cleanly through his hand, perfectly "filleting" it, and there wasn't a single drop of blood.

Fortunately for him, there just happened to be a large destroyer tender from the US Navy in port, the USS Dixie, with a fully equipped hospital. What a stroke of luck! Brian was lucky enough to be patched up in the ship, much to the relief of his parents, or he would have faced being medevacked to Nairobi by plane. The USS Dixie, which had been brought into service just before the start of WW2, was on its way home to the US to be decommissioned after 42 years of service and indeed, in 1981, it was awarded the First Navy Jack for being the longest active service in the US Navy. It had witnessed the ebbs and flows of history, an honoured recipient of the First Navy Jack for its unmatched dedication.

Warsheikh is an important historical Islamic centre and has been a centre of trade and learning in the region. It was one of the principal settlements of the Sultanate of Mogadishu during the Middle Ages.

The town has an old mosque situated near a cape, which features an inscription noting its construction in 1278H (1861-1862 CE) by Sheikh Abu Bakr b. Mihzar b. Ahmad al-Kasadi. The masjid has three rows of transverse, east-west piers and a foliate mihrab, standing as a testament to time. It also has attached chambers, with the Sheikh's tomb situated in an adjacent room.

According to local oral tradition, the place name '*Warsheik*' originated from holy men seeking to propagate Islam within Somalia. The fable goes that having become parched following a lengthy expedition, they lifted their hands in prayer, beseeching Allah for the gift of water. Their prayers were not in vain; in close proximity, they spotted water splattering upon the earth. Having quenched their thirst, they encountered a nomadic household and enquired about food and shelter. However, the family claimed a lack of water for meal preparation. The scholar assured them, directing them to the newfound water source. They discovered the water where the scholar had indicated, leading others in the village to question the source of her water-filled container. The family revealed that the instructions came from the sheikh; thus, the term '*Warsheik*', was born –

'*Warkii*' symbolising 'information' and '*Sheekha*' denoting 'religious scholar'.

Despite the fable, as was the case forty years ago, water continues to this day a major problem for the local community given the very low water table.

Warsheikh also reached notoriety in April 1890 when off the coast local Somalis killed two Italian seafarers, Lieutenant Carlo Zavagli and Captain Angelo Bartorello. This act led to the first Italian colonial naval bombardment in Somalia in retaliation.

For us, the area was very special, and whilst we kept some distance from the local community out of respect, Warsheikh was a calm and beautiful spot on the Somali coast.

Despite being restricted in travelling no further north than Warsheikh and no further south than Merka, we were exceptionally lucky with the allure of various beaches at our disposal, a coastline revealing a treasure trove of beauty waiting to be explored. Reverting to my initial point, people could see the real beauty of Somalia from a sea and coastal perspective. They would have a significantly different and perhaps unprejudiced view of Somalia. The salty breeze caressed our faces as we gazed out onto the vast expanse of the ocean, a canvas of endless possibilities. From the sea and coastal perspective, Somalia unfurled its true essence - a land of contrasts and hidden gems that defied the prevailing prejudices. However, there are still many contradictions and realities. Amidst the scenic splendour, the contradictions and realities of Somalia's complex landscape were undeniable. The echoes of a turbulent history reverberated through the land, leaving scars that time could not fully heal.

Chapter 7 - Istunka

We headed off to Afgooye just after lunch, and I recall that it was still rather warm and hardly the climate for any fight, let alone a stick fight. What do they say about *only mad dogs and Englishmen going out in the midday sun*…….and we felt very out of place!

Dabshid or the lighting of the fire is a pre-Islamic festival and heralds the beginning of a new Somali solar calendar or more specifically a new farming year (It falls on either the 27th or 28th of July). The *Dabshid* festival, also known in Somali as *Neyruz*, is a pre-Islamic festival of supposedly Persian heritage. Whilst there is no direct link between the Persian Zoroastrian festival of *Nowruz*, from which *Neyruz* takes its name, it is a key event on the Somalia farming calendar.

Dabshid has been occurring for millennia and is to wish for a successful farming season ahead. Somalis, as all Muslims, follow the lunar year, however, farmers use the solar year for the timing of crops and livestock husbandry. During *Dabshid* bonfires are built and men participate in stick fighting or *Istunka* and tribal dancing.

Dabshid reminds me so much of the May Day or 'Obby 'Oss Festival in Padstow in Cornwall on the 1st of May which is an old pagan Celtic religious ritual designed to secure fertility and welcome the approach of summer again with two competing sides - the Old Oss and the Blue Ribbon Oss.

Istunka, also known as "*Laambad*" or "stick fighting," is a traditional combat sport and cultural practice associated with the Somali people. It involves two participants engaging in a physical confrontation using long sticks or rods as weapons. This ancient combat sport ignited a fiery spirit among the participants, their eyes gleaming with determination as they wielded long sticks, ready to engage in the age-old dance of strength and skill. The objective is to strike the opponent while avoiding being hit oneself. It wasn't just a physical confrontation but a display of courage, an art form that melded athleticism with tradition.

Stick fighting has been a long-standing tradition in many African cultures, including Somalia, and serves various purposes, such as entertainment, physical conditioning, and a way to demonstrate bravery and skill. It often takes place during festive occasions, ceremonies, or traditional festivals, preserving a heritage that connects them to their roots. This was more than just a sport; it was a celebration of identity and the art of storytelling through physical expression. However, it's important to note that Somali society is diverse, and customs can vary across different regions and communities within Somalia.

Stick fighting, or *istunka*, is not inherently connected to pagan religious beliefs. Rather, it is a cultural practice and traditional sport that has historical roots in Somali society. While some aspects of Somali culture may have pre-Islamic influences, it's essential to note that the majority of the Somali population is Muslim, and Islam is the predominant religion in Somalia. Stick fighting is primarily viewed as a cultural tradition rather than a religious practice, where the rhythmic clash of sticks paints a picture of bravery and unity.

However, in the shadows of the present-day struggle against extremist ideologies, it is hard to believe today that in the context of Al Shabaab or Islamic State that these traditions and ways of life ever existed, and entirely conceivable that many have either just disappeared due to draconian extremist Islamist rule or just through accommodation by the local people to avoid being targeted by an Al Shabaab spy or informer. Even then, you were always watched and observed. The once vibrant streets filled with the sounds of celebrations, are now and have been from some time stifled by the ominous presence of surveillance and informants.

In a convoy of two Land Rovers, my Dad's V8 and the Overseas Development Agency (ODA) Long Wheel Base Series 2, we headed off down the Afgooye Road for the 40 kilometres that led us to the River Shebelle and the village of Afgooye.

In addition to being a key strategic crossing to the south of Somalia as well as to Baodoa and Merka, Afgooye was a richly cultivated area with abundantly thriving guava, bananas and grapefruit. The fruit was indeed a key export from the country, and so the river held significant importance to not only the local population of farmers but the country as a whole.

When you arrive in Mogadishu, you are greeted by a real aridness, and yet only a short journey away, you are transported to an oasis of lushness and cool shade. The river was a dark brown and looked like chocolate and was full of alluvium. Indeed, it was also full of nasties such as Bilharzia, a malicious parasite that lurked within its depths. So pretty to look at but not advisable to swim or wash in. Indeed, a friend of my dad's had been working on an ODA project in the area, had unwittingly washed in the river, and sadly contracted the disease. By the time he was diagnosed, it was too late, and his liver was riddled with the parasite. I do recall my dad helping him onto a Somali Airlines flight home, to sadly die as his condition was terminal. His liver was so enlarged with parasites that he cradled it while boarding the aircraft — a very sad sight.

Crossing the river over the Italian equivalent of a Bailey bridge, we pulled into an area about the size of two football fields connected widthways. You could feel the excitement and trepidation in the air. The village of Afgooye straddled the River Shebelle, and on either side of the river lived two tribes, with the open area serving as a meeting point. Again, this was in the context of a political environment where tribalism was outlawed. Each year the tribes would meet at this open area in a contest that would bestow on the winner good fortune and, importantly, a good harvest. In this spirited event, the tribes would compete to bestow the victor with blessings of prosperity and a bountiful harvest. It was a celebration of unity, where the boundaries of tribal identities blurred, and a sense of shared heritage prevailed.

When we arrived, we could position the vehicles adjacent to the open field, and clambering onto the roofs of the Land Rovers provided an elevated vantage point. We didn't know what to expect, but you could feel the anticipation hung in the air like an electric charge, much like you would sense at a football cup final. The village open field, now the arena for this ancient contest, brimmed with both intensity and mystery. With every passing moment, the atmosphere intensified. The two opposing sides, like gladiators preparing for battle, channelled their focus and energy.

The field echoed with the sounds of singing and chanting, adding to the fervour of the occasion. At some point, the umpires and village elders appeared and, as masters of ceremonies, spoke to representatives of each side. As stick fights go, things seemed very reserved. Amid the excitement, an air of formality pervaded as the elders inspected the sticks, ensuring they met the regulations - a size and width that would allow for fierce competition without causing permanent harm and certainly not of a size that would put said combatants in hospital - not that there was one for miles and miles. I should point out that this was entirely a male pursuit, and women served no role in the fighting.

No sooner had the elders left the field, and then chaos ensued. Chaos erupted like a tempest. A flurry of acrid dust flew, and all that was visible was a ball of dust, sticks flying, and men going about the battle. I think it was at that moment that my parents questioned the wisdom of attending such a spectacle. However, we were in too deep now, and it was impossible to back out.

Amidst the whirlwind of sticks and dust, the battle seemed relentless, the unyielding warriors continuing their fight with an unwavering spirit. The echoes of the combat reverberated across the field as the struggle persisted for what felt like an eternity. Grown men continued to beat one another with sticks. This went on unrelenting for at least ten minutes before the event took a turn, and suddenly men on each side started to dig with their bare hands and pull up pre-planned heavier and more dangerous sticks that were designed to inflict more damage. Now men started to fall as they were cracked over their heads, collapsing with concussion and blood streaming down their heads. The mood took a darker turn, and the once controlled stick fights now transformed into a brutal melee. It was at this point you could see men being carried off to be tended to by the women of their corresponding tribe. The field was now a landscape of both victory and sorrow, where the echoes of celebration and pain coalesced. It became evident that the line between sport and peril had blurred, a moment that left you questioning what was going on and, in particular, the toll it took on some of its participants.

In the thrilling world of *Istunka*, the path to victory is one of skill, endurance, and sportsmanship and not just brute force and who has the largest stick. While there might be slight variations in different regions or communities, the following aspects generally contribute to deciding the victor:

1. Skill and Technique: The primary consideration in determining the winner of *Istunka* is the skill and technique displayed by the participants. Like artisans of combat, they showcase their mastery in handling the sticks, their every move calculated and purposeful. Judges or onlookers assess the fighters' agility, speed, accuracy, and overall proficiency in handling the sticks. Clean strikes, effective defensive manoeuvres, and strategic, graceful footwork are often key factors in evaluating the fighters' abilities.

2. Endurance and Stamina: *Istunka* bouts can be physically demanding, testing the fighters' endurance and stamina. The ability to maintain a high level of energy and focus throughout the fight is highly valued. A fighter who demonstrates remarkable endurance, lasting power, and resilience, even in the face of fatigue, may gain an advantage in judging.

3. Offensive Strikes and Defence: Successful offensive strikes and effective defensive techniques play a crucial role in determining the winner. Judges take into account the number of clean hits landed on the opponent as well as the ability to dodge or block incoming strikes. A fighter with well-executed attacks and skilful defence is likely to be favoured in the evaluation.

4. Sportsmanship and Conduct: The conduct and sportsmanship of the fighters also contribute to the judging process. The fighters, like guardians of a noble legacy, embody the values of *Istunka* with every move they make. Participants are expected to adhere to the rules and etiquette of *Istunka*, showing respect towards their opponents and the tradition itself. Unsportsmanlike behaviour, such as excessive aggression, intentional fouls, or disrespectful actions, may result in penalties or even disqualification, for *Istunka* is not just a sport but a reflection of the honour and dignity that define the Somali people.

5. Crowd Response: The reaction of the spectators can have an influence on the determination of the winner. The crowd's enthusiasm, applause, and vocal support for a particular fighter can sway the judgment of the judges. However, it's important to note that crowd response is not the sole determining factor and is generally considered alongside the other aspects mentioned.

It's essential to remember that *Istunka* is deeply rooted in Somali culture and traditions, and the specifics of determining the winner may vary depending on the particular region or community where the stick fight takes place. The aim is to recognise and appreciate fighters' skills, technique, and overall performance, ensuring a fair and engaging competition.

The fighting went on until it was clear that one side had unanimously won the battle, and the opposing side slunk off. The aftermath painted a scene of both triumph and resilience, with men murmuring in pain and being tended to with immediate first aid. The battlefield bore witness to the true cost of *Istunka*, a testament to the dedication and passion that coursed through the veins of the participants.

Aside from the physical toll, our Somali host revealed that this rite of passage and fertility battle had a deeper significance. The victorious went home, emboldened by their conquest, ready to consummate their victory, and the losing side and injured were nursed similarly, acknowledging the shared bond of being part of a timeless tradition. Whether it really did anything for the fertility of their crops is entirely questionable. But you can perhaps understand that such pagan traditions, despite Islam, still held an important social component and had been a long-standing tradition for many generations before Islam itself.

When we could free ourselves from the hustle and bustle of the open field, we slowly drove back to Mogadishu and perhaps in shock. We had witnessed something quite violent but equally just accepted it as something not part of our tradition or way of life. It is hard to relate to when it is not part of your culture or heritage but as something I witnessed, I feel now as an adult immensely honoured and privileged.

Looking at the stick fights of Afgooye objectively, you could say that they were examples of man at his most basic, and whether it's fighting with sticks or modern weapons, man has been fighting for strategic supremacy since the dawn of time. Whether wielding sticks or modern weapons, the thirst for strategic dominance seemed woven into the very fabric of human history, transcending cultures and generations, and certainly seems to have been the case in Somali history.

Now in 2023 and given the control and presence of Al Shabaab in Banadir, Lower Shabelle, and Hiraan regions, I wonder if such traditions continue to be practised and to what degree. I would imagine that in the thirty or so years since the Civil War and the Islamisation of Somalia, these traditions may be gone and dead and buried, becoming casualties of a changing landscape.

Yet, somewhere in the heart of Somalia, in the whispers of memories passed down through generations, the spirit of *Istunka* and other cultural traditions may linger. Even in the face of adversity, there is an indomitable resilience that characterizes the Somali people, a spirit that refuses to be entirely erased.

I frequently look at the photographs that my dad took of the people of Afgooye, you are transported back in time, reliving the moments of the stick fights in Afgooye, and despite the superficial brutality of the annual stick fight, people looked happy, at peace and content. People smiled and were open and welcoming. The images tell a story of a community bonded by tradition, where joy and camaraderie prevailed amidst the intensity of the battle. Indeed there was a softness, and whilst they were Muslims, there was no religious separation of men and women. Men and women coexisted freely, their lives interwoven in a tapestry of vibrant colours and ties to their fertile land. It was a portrait of a culture that embraced life's diversity, unencumbered by the rigid divisions that would come to characterize later times.

The memories of Afgooye, now forty years distant, fill you with wonder and amazement that such a tradition existed even then. In a rapidly changing world, the survival of such ancient traditions seems almost miraculous. So much of the modern world has killed off pagan traditions that predate modern man. Yet, in the heart of Afgooye, you saw a living testament to the enduring strength of cultural heritage. I can still taste the earthy dust and visualise sticks flying, not that it negatively played on my mind but as an observer of bygone traditions.

Sadly, it is only through memories that you can recollect *Istunka* and celebrate the resilience of the people who once graced the battlefield as, perhaps unusually, my Dad didn't take any photographs. Aside from anything else, it would have been highly disrespectful and equally marked with suspicion. Many men fighting would now be in the late sixties and seventies. I wonder how many of them are still alive today or have fallen victim to the Civil War and the brutality of the extremism that followed. As you reflect on the past, you also acknowledge the present, where the echoes of Afgooye's traditions may still ripple through the hearts of those who carry its legacy.

Woman collecting water from the River Shabelle in Afgooye

Chapter 8 - Dining Out on the Afgooye Road

It is perhaps not surprising that in a country with extreme food scarcity, the notion of "dining out" was very rare and indeed a luxury. Most of the few restaurants at the time were either in hotels, at embassy locations or at the infamous Liido Club. So generally, from an expat basis, we didn't eat out, rather went to each other's houses for a barbeque or went to the beach for a barbeque. Food was a luxurious and precious commodity on any level. At the time, most food with the exception of local produce, such as bananas, guava, and grapefruit, was imported. But on the whole most of the local produce was, in fact, for export, and something that has stuck with me is the heavy trucks, called in Somali "*kalibracey*", would thunder down the Afgooye Road heading for the port and an awaiting boat to take the refrigerated product to another geography.

At the time, the Soviet Union was still in existence and given Somalia's then-socialist leanings, food was imported or donated from the Eastern Bloc. We enjoyed such delights as Bulgarian strawberry jam! The memory of those flavours linger on today, a reminder of a bygone era when international politics and influences left their mark on our local diet. Of course, given the Italian colonial heritage there was also pasta!

However, it would be very wrong to say that there were no restaurants, and as our time in Mogadishu passed, more and more new restaurants opened up, including a pizza takeaway.

One notable restaurant memorable to many Somalis who lived in Mogadishu before 1991 was the Araf Restaurant, which was also known as The Jungle Restaurant, on Afgooye Road. It was a short distance from our house and just off the road that extended from Mogadishu to Afgooye.

I only visited the restaurant once but it was extremely memorable. As the memories of the Araf Restaurant resurface, I find myself journeying back to a time when life was simpler and the essence of community was woven into the fabric of every gathering. Given the challenges of food scarcity and the importance of social dynamics, the joy of coming together to savour a meal and share moments of celebration remains a cherished memory, a testament to the resilience and spirit of the Somali people.

The restaurant was of rudimentary construction, essentially built around a few acacia trees, which served a dual purpose. Bush hedging provided a barrier and effectively cordoned off the restaurant from the surrounding scrub. As with every property in Somalia, there was a clear and distinct delineation between the bush and the restaurant, and through a gap, you would drive off the road and into the restaurant. The restaurant was particularly popular for religious festivals and celebrations such as funerals and marriages, but again, these were exclusively male-only affairs.

Under most of the trees at the Araf Restaurant was a large plastic mat which provided not only respite for weary restaurant-goers but also "the table" off which we would eat. The first purpose of the tree was to provide some shade under which restaurant-goers could take off their shoes and sit under the mat and await food. From memory this restaurant had a very limited menu and specialised in one classic dish, *Hilib Ari Duban* or in English spice encrusted roast goat meat. Goat or specifically kid goat meat is a popular meat amongst the primarily nomadic Somali people who savour the soft, juicy taste. Goats are a sustainable animal to farm and can endure drought tolerant conditions which make them ideally suited to the semi-arid environment of Somalia. Somalia has its own breed of goat called the *deg yar* which has short ears and white hair sometimes with dark patches.

It befell the person typically paying to perform the duty of selecting a kid goat from a small corral close to the food preparation area. Once the kid had been selected, the chef would climb into the pen and hold the kid between his legs with precision and purpose, holding the head of the animal in his left hand and a sharp knife in his right and quickly cut the animal's throat. There would initially be much commotion, and then an eerie silence would follow at which point the animal was losing its life. Its rear legs would be tied together, and then in another acacia tree, it would be strung up. The animal was pulled up just high enough that its body was not touching the floor and high enough for the chef to start preparing the animal for the fire. Initially, the animal was left, and the blood was allowed to drain from its body. I should point out that at this stage, there was an abundance of flies. The stomach cavity was opened, and the entrails were carefully removed. The skin was then also carefully dissected from the animal until effectively all that was left was meat and bone. I don't actually recall the blood being kept, but I do recall certain offal delicacies being put to one side.

Carefully the animal was lowered, and a wooden stake was then passed through the animal from end to end, and it was tied to the stake with the legs also tied together. The animal was then placed on a rudimentary frame over the fire and left to cook.

Meanwhile, in the kitchen, as the meat was cooking over the fire, its succulent aroma mingling with the surrounding acacia trees, white rice would be prepared in a large vat in the makeshift kitchen. I honestly don't recall any other food items being prepared, not even bread. Given that going out to a restaurant was an extremely rare occasion, we would be invited to drink some tea. Instead, the rarity of dining out transformed the experience into something more than just a meal; it became a cherished moment of connection and friendship. Again the notion of soft drinks was alien and a very rare event so I don't believe we had anything like that. The tea was made with sugar and was very sweet to the taste – far too much sugar for my palate!

As the anticipation built, the wait felt like an eternity, but it was worth it; as the saying goes, *good things come to those who wait*! After a few hours of chatting, there was suddenly a hive of activity. The meat was ready, and so was the rice. On our large mat, the vat of cooked rice was tipped onto it. A massive mountain of steaming white rice! I don't think I have personally ever seen that volume of rice cooked since. A few moments later, the meat was carefully brought over and similarly tipped over the rice. The meat was extremely tender and broke over the rice quite easily.

We were gathered around the edge of the mat with the plentiful rice in the middle of the circle, creating a truly communal dining experience. The mat was not only for our benefit to keep us off the ground but was essentially a very large plate holding our food. I have been to many communal meals in different countries, but this was by far and away the most communal. There was then a discussion about the meat and which parts of the animal to tear off and consume. Religion dictated that we entirely ate with our right hands, and there was to be no use of the left. Furthermore, there were no more than hands to tear at the meat. No utensils and no knives. The idea was to tear off a piece of meat and carefully roll it with some rice into a small mouth-sized ball and then eat it. There was a lot of politeness also encouraging your neighbour to eat the best part of the animal. For me personally, the best piece of the animal was the rib cage. I recall the delicately flavoured meat around the small ribs, which were a little bigger than a chicken wing. Everyone ate until they were sated. I can't really remember anything being wasted. Understandably food wastage was a big no-no given the extreme poverty that existed and I am sure it is very much the same today.

After the goat meal we were served more sweet tea and plates of chopped banana and guava were passed around. This effectively marked the end of the dining experience and we left and went our separate ways.

This event aside, I have to be entirely honest. As a consequence of the event and perhaps as a direct result of seeing the animal dramatically dispatched and butchered, I can't now eat goat or any goat products. Indeed, eating goat's cheese today immediately takes me back to the Afar Restaurant. Whilst there is perhaps no fur at all in what I am eating, I can still taste it in the back of my throat. While the association is entirely psychosomatic, it's a testament to the powerful impact of experiences on our perceptions and preferences, and it is amazing how an episode forty years ago has continued to have an effect on me today. Again, I mean no disrespect to any Somalis. I suppose I am just one of those people that don't like goat meat.

As far as I am aware, the Araf Restaurant existed for a number of years after our departure but, like many things, it most likely disappeared altogether. However, even after forty years the memory of the restaurant is strong. What I liked about it was the coming together and communal nature of enjoying what is a unique culinary tradition.

Chapter 9 - A road trip to Buur Heybe

Somalia is a country of many paradoxes. As we press on, the road seems to stretch into infinity, bordered by a vast expanse of orange sand and dotted with hardy acacia bushes. Driving through Afgooye, you can only be struck by the verdant beauty of the River Shabelle meandering through the village and the lush green foliage of the overhanging trees and plants. A stark contrast to the arid bushland that envelopes it.

As we continue our journey the tarmac stretches out from Mogadishu to Afgooye and then the road bends to the north and passes over an old prefabricated, portable truss bridge across the River Shabelle. Once over the bridge, which looks like it was a remnant of colonial occupation, the tarmac continues in a northerly direction and soon the fertile green of Afgooye ends. We are back out into the arid bushland again that characterises much of Somalia.

The tarmac, though a welcome sight, is far from perfect. It bears the marks of time and wear, riddled with potholes that jostle us along the way. The scenery is a very repetitive pattern of orange sand and acacia bushes as if nature itself plays a broken record of earthy hues. At this time, there weren't many tarmacked roads and in this remote corner of the world it was no less than a luxury. This particular road went to Baidoa and from there to Luuq on the Somali - Ethiopian border. The route is extremely straightforward as it is a lifeline of connectivity for trade and transport. We just had to follow the road.

After a short distance from Afgooye, we pass through the town of Wanlaweyn. The town itself was eerily deserted and the scene was very reminiscent of a Spaghetti Western where time stands still and the ghosts of the past seem to linger in the still air. The absence of tumbleweed and John Wayne is all that's missing to complete this surreal cinematic-like experience. After driving for two hours we pulled over to the side of the road for a quick coffee in the desolate setting. We were literally in the middle of nowhere amidst this vast wilderness.

After a brief stop our journey continues and the road turns and heads north-west and we continue for another hour and a half until we reach

Burhakaba. We pass very few vehicles as the road is mainly used by diesel trucks loaded with sugar cane or bananas heading to the port. Other than that we are entirely alone on the road. The tarmac may be imperfect, the scenery repetitive, but every mile carries us closer to the essence of this paradoxical country. In the simplicity of following the road we find the freedom to explore, uncover the secrets of this enigmatic land and embrace the solitude that makes this journey a truly unforgettable adventure.

As we leave the tarmac behind and venture into the unknown the desert track leads us northeast, guided by the well-worn tracks etched by those who came before us. The destination remains somewhat mysterious but the clarity of the path assures us we are on the right course. With every kilometre covered the anticipation grows, knowing that something remarkable lies ahead.

Burhakaba is a relatively large town on the road to Baidoa. The town is in a wide valley known as '*Bohol Wiinti*" that runs through the town from the north, east, and south-east. At Burhakaba we leave the tarmac and head in a north-easterly direction on a desert track. It's not entirely clear where we are heading but given the well-furrowed track marks, we were confident that we were on the right path. Buur Haybe is about 30 kilometres from Burhakaba and as we approach we can see in the distance this mountainous outcrop appears on the horizon and begin to grow and grow as we get closer and closer.

By the time my Dad and I reached Buur Heybe we were pretty exhausted, and we arrived at camp just after lunchtime. It was evident that meticulous organization and care have gone into maintaining this safe haven amidst the rugged wilderness. The camp was extremely well organised and very clean and tidy. Our visit was only for 24 hours but every moment was precious as we immersed ourselves in the splendour of this extraordinary place and Dad had a clear photographic task to perform. Mum had stayed behind in Mogadishu with my younger siblings.

I left my Dad who was talking with Dr Steven Brandt, an eminent archaeologist, and I went for a wander in the surrounding jungle with one of the young archaeologists. What I hadn't appreciated was that there was a natural water source at Buur Heybe Hill. Surrounded by the sounds of the jungle we basked in the feeling of being connected to the natural world. The whispers of the wind, the rustling leaves, and the distant calls of wildlife formed a soothing symphony that lulled us into a sense of serenity. It was a very different natural environment to our home in Mogadishu. The hill itself was a large granite mound and around it were natural springs. We climbed into the wooded area on top of the hill. This was boys' own stuff and we were following a path that had been cleared through the dense undergrowth.

Eventually, we reached the top of the mound and were able to look down to the dig site below, hidden and protected by a large granite boulder that had broken over it, and the track which had brought us into Bur Heybe running towards Buurhakaba which we could not see from our vantage point. What I hadn't appreciated at the time but was subsequently told later was the young German archaeologist who had taken me to the top of the Bur Haybe hill was actually an East German and he had successfully scaled the Berlin Wall without being shot or captured and had escaped to freedom in West Germany.

We returned to camp, where Dad was now busy taking photographs of the dig site. As the evening sun approached we prepared our sleeping area. The camp was so well set up that all we had to get out were our sleeping bags. We had camp cots already set up in a fly netted sleeping area, unfurled our sleeping bags and cosied up for a night under the starry Somali sky. There was a separate kitchen area in the camp where food and meals were prepared. In the evening we had a barbeque on the open fire around which we sat keeping warm. Before long the aroma of a barbeque wafted through the camp, drawing us together around the open fire. The flickering flames danced to the rhythm of the night casting light on our faces as we shared stories and experiences and illuminating the rocks behind us. In this remote corner of Somalia, gathered around the fire, we felt a kinship with the land and with one another, united by a shared sense of wonder and exploration.

After dinner we headed off to sleep. As the night deepened we bid each other goodnight and retreated to our respective sleeping areas. The camp was peaceful, cocooned by the enveloping darkness and the sounds of nature settling in for the night. The rhythmic chirping of cicada, the cooing of the Somali stock pigeons and the distant hoot of an indigenous Little Owl accompanied us into a restful slumber.

Naturally sleeping outdoors we were woken by the daylight that filtered through the lush jungle canopy. My Dad, a steadfast coffee enthusiast, was quick to indulge in his morning ritual before immersing himself in photographing the fascinating dig site below the broken granite boulder. It was truly an impressive sight. In the dig site, which was underneath this broken granite boulder, were a number of skeletons. The neolithic skeletons bore witness to a time long before ours, and their mysterious traditions left a profound impression on those who uncovered them. Among the artifacts was a peculiar mound of collected teeth which stood as a testament to the customs of these ancient people, a ritual of significance now long lost in the sands of time.

Buur Heybe literally means *'hill of the potter's sand'*, and what the various archaeological digs have shown is that there has been some form of inhabitants there for more than 30,000 years. The first archaeological dig was during the Italian occupation of Somalia by Paolo Graziosi in the 1930s in the rock shelter site. There were then further excavations by J. Desmond Clark in the 1950s and then subsequently Dr Steven Brandt's Buur Ecological and Archaeological Project (BEAP) in the 1980s. Steven was supported at the dig site by his wife, Melanie, and a team of archaeologists from Somalia and abroad. Dad had been contracted to take photographs of the dig for Steven.

In the countryside, far from the bustling city of Mogadishu, life unfolded in its own unique way. Ancient customs existed in their own right, as many customs and traditions. Islamic practices coexisted with practical necessities, resulting in customs and traditions that might not be deemed orthodox but were deeply rooted in the traditions of daily life. Being that far from civilisation, you could have been practically anywhere, and that perhaps explains why certain traditions that maybe deamed by some as 'unIslamic' naturally co-exist. They were traditions built around the environment and for the necessity of life. They were also highly practical and efficient.

Amidst the ancient hills of Buur Heybe, my Dad's camera lens captured a striking image of a proud hunter adorned in a simple white t-shirt and a sarong fashioned into makeshift shorts. With an air of pride, he embodied the spirit of the Somali hunters of old. A pack of lean and swift Somali dogs, akin to the renowned Saluki breed, accompanied him, their loyalty a testament to the bond between man and beast.

The hunter's craft was an art passed down through generations. He would set up his nets in a line across a well-worn animal trail and then, with deft precision, would use the dogs to chase small antelope towards the nets where they would become entangled. The hunter then would either target them with a spear or a bow and arrow, dispatching the animal immediately. Somali antelopes are called dik-dik and are about the size of a baby deer.

In a seamless display of skill and reverence, the hunter would approach the captured dik-dik. He would then set about dismantling the animal's body, ensuring a humane and immediate end to its life. The skin would be stretched on a wooden frame and cured in the sun. The meat would be either traded for something more valuable or stored in cloth for future consumption. The dik-dik's body held great value to the hunter, not only for sustenance but also for trade. Each part was thoughtfully utilized, paying homage to the age-old tradition of honouring nature's gifts.

Again, the use of hunting dogs was another time-old tradition and in contrast to the way the city dwellers of Mogadishu treated dogs. For them, dogs were viewed as embodiments of the devil. The innocent animals were often subject to harsh treatment and often stoned by the hands of prying children.

Indeed, the stick fight of Afgooye and the hunting with dogs in Bur Heybe are just two examples of the rich tapestry of ancient traditions that have existed in Somalia for millennia. As time passed and the world evolved, these customs gradually faded into the annals of history, leaving behind cherished memories and a profound connection to a bygone era. These are only a couple of examples, and no doubt, in the intervening twenty to thirty years, many others have just disappeared into history.

After our eye opening and educational experience in Bur Heybe, we reluctantly bid farewell to the archaeological dig site and headed back to Mogadishu in our trusty Land Rover. I don't remember much about the return journey at all, but it felt like we had been to another country and was so different from our lives in Mogadishu, the memories of the lush greenery and ancient hills blending into a nostalgic haze as we re-entered civilisation.

However, those return visits to Buur Heybe offered a chance to revisit a past that spanned thousands of years. Each time we ventured back, it was as if the veil of time lifted, and we were transported to a realm untouched by modernity. Amongst the granite mounds and natural springs, we felt an undeniable connection to the ancestors who once roamed those lands.

As we traversed through the arid bush and orange sands, we couldn't help but marvel at the enduring spirit of Somalia. It was a land that held within its soil the stories of countless generations, each contributing to the unique tapestry of its cultural heritage.

Yet, we also acknowledged the bittersweet truth that some of these ancient customs had slipped away into history, lost in the sands of time. The stick fight of Afgooye, the hunting with dogs in Bur Heybe, and so many other practices were echoes of a distant past and most likely now preserved in memory only.

View of Buur Heybe from top of the 'Hill of the Potters Sand'

Buur Heybe dig site

Buur Heybe dig site

Neolithic skeletons at Buur Heybe

The hunter with his nets

Chapter 10 - Mogadishu Old

I could see Mogadishu below me, like a small blinding-white wedding cake on the burned brown sand, the blue ocean lapping at its edges.

(Gerald Hanley)

Mogadishu is fittingly referred to as the 'White Pearl' on the Indian Ocean. What first strikes you on arriving is the whitewashed buildings set against the azure blue of the sea, forming a stunning contrast against the deep blue expanse of the Indian Ocean. The brilliance of the white hues can be so overwhelming that it almost feels like the city is welcoming you with its radiant glow. In 1983 this white pearl was at its prime with immaculate buildings and well-maintained streets that were pristine, exuding a sense of order and elegance. Sadly, whilst much remains over the past thirty years, a lot of the buildings have either been destroyed or fallen into disrepair.

The modern part of the city reflects thoughtful urban planning and design, with wide avenues adorned by neatly trimmed palm trees casting their shadows over well-paved roads. The streets are alive with the buzz of commerce, vibrant markets, and bustling cafes where locals and visitors alike engage in lively conversations. The architecture showcases a blend of modern styles and influences, with echoes of Italian colonial influences adding a unique charm to the cityscape.

In addition to this very modern and planned city are the intermingled districts of Hamar Weyne and Shangani, which have been in existence in one form or another for many hundreds of years. Here, you'll find buildings that have withstood the test of time, standing as living monuments of the city's historied past. The narrow alleys and stone streets echo tales of generations past, with each corner revealing glimpses of historical landmarks and traditional homes that have been passed down through the same families for centuries. Mogadishu is in the southeastern Banadir region of Somalia.

Hamar Weyne

Hamar or *Xamar* in Somali means tamarind tree of which in the country there was an abundance. Tamarind comes from the Arabic word *tamar hind* or 'Indian wood' and is a spice used in Indian and East African cooking and can also be boiled to make tea.

In Hamar Weyne (in Somali D*egmada Xamar Weynes*) the aromas of spices and freshly baked bread fill the air, beckoning you to explore the vibrant markets where local traders display their colourful array of goods. It has a number of notable buildings, namely *Jama'a Hamar Weyne*, which holds the distinction of being the oldest of the three mosques on the entire east coast of Africa and was built in 1238 AD (636 AH). Its age is awe-inspiring and stepping down into the mosque's prayer hall gives you a sense of entering a sacred space that has been a place of worship for centuries. The floor of the mosque is about two metres below street level and stair access is required to access the prayer hall, adding a touch of grandeur to the mosque's architectural design. The mosque is also known locally by another name: Mohamed Al Awal or Mohamed the First, and was built during the reign of Mohamed Ali, which adds a historical layer to its already significant existence.

The other building of note in Hamar Weyne and the second oldest mosque is the Fakr ad-Din Mosque (*Masjid Fakhr Ad-Din*). The mosque is identifiable by its unique design, characterized by two striking cones, one round and the other hexagonal sets it apart from other structures in the vicinity. It was built by Sultan Abu Bake Fakr ad-Din, the first Sultan of the Sultanate of Mogadishu, which reflects the rich architectural prowess of its time. The building is primarily made of coral and marble and the mosque's rectangular shape domed mihrab creates a sense of serenity and sacredness. Glazed tiles were used to decorate the mihrab and one bears a dated inscription showcasing intricate craftsmanship and artistic finesse. It was built in 1269 AD (667 AH), thirty years after *Jama'a Hamar Weyne*.

Shangani

Shangani (in Somali *Degmada Shangaani)* is home to the other third oldest mosque in East Africa, namely *Arbaca Rukun,* which was built in the same year as the Fakr ad-Din Mosque in 1269 AD (667 AH). The Arbaca Rukun Mosque (known as *Jama'a Arba'a Rukun* in Arabic) is a place of great reverence and significance for the local community. Its distinguished mihrab, the focal point of the mosque, bears inscriptions that harken back to the very moment of its construction, commemorating the mosque's esteemed founder, Khusra Ibn Mubarak Al-Shirazi. As you step into the prayer hall the inscriptions on the mihrab serve as a historical bridge transporting you back in time to a period of great importance and religious devotion.

The mosque's architecture showcases a seamless blend of artistic finesse and spiritual significance. As you explore its interior you can't help but be captivated by the craftsmanship displayed in every intricate detail. The mosque's design reflects the prevailing architectural style of the era, and its enduring elegance is a testament to the skilled artisans who dedicated themselves to its construction.

Life in Shangani

I was fortunate to have a local friend at school called Zainab who unusually actually lived in Shangani. Her family were from a long-established trading family that had originated from what is today Pakistan but had traded with Somalia for generations prior to Partition. I say fortunate because we were taken on a tour of Shangani and visited her home, which on the whole was unusual. Being centuries old the streets and alleys were not as straight as the more formal colonial Italianate roads and streets of the newer part of the city, but you had a real sense of community with people living close to one another, side by side. It was very different to our own existence stuck out in the middle of nowhere on the Afgooye Road.

The buildings in Shangani were centuries old. They were like living relics, embodying the architectural legacy of Mogadishu's past. Made from coral and mortar they stood proudly with their weathered facades bearing witness to the passage of time. Each two-story structure exuded a sense of history and permanence, standing tall as silent witnesses to the countless lives that resided within their walls. When stepping inside, you are greeted by the warm hospitality and timeless simplicity of the interiors. The inside was rudimentary with a dining area and a small but functional kitchen off of it and a large seating area on the ground floor. The large seating area was the heart of the home, a space where stories were exchanged, laughter echoed, and memories were made. Wooden stairs to the side of the structure took you up to the first floor, where there were the bedrooms and an upstairs bathroom and shower, the latter being a modern addition. Finally, a further set of wooden stairs took you up to the roof, which was an memorable experience. The flat roof offered a unique vantage point from which to observe the city below. As you sat surrounded by the gentle breeze you could feel the rhythm of Mogadishu's heartbeat. From this perch the rich tapestry of life unfolded below you — the bustling streets, the vibrant markets, and the timeless beauty of the Indian Ocean lapping at the city's Liido shores. The building had no air conditioning. However, the lack of air conditioning was hardly a concern, as the gentle coastal breeze and the strategically positioned fans provided a refreshing respite from the heat, especially during the cool nights when the rooftop terrace became a haven of comfort and relaxation. Whilst at Zainab's house we were treated to a cup of sweet black tea and a spicey hot vegetable samosa which again seemed like a novelty. It was very generous of her family given our number.

    The construction of the upper floor was a sight to behold. Sitting and having my samosa I looked up and could see the construction of the floor above. The beams were made of trunks of palm trees, which served as a testament to the resourcefulness of the local builders, who skilfully utilized the natural materials available to them. You could easily spot the corrugation of the palm tree bark, which showcased the raw beauty of this organic support system, reflecting the harmony between man and nature that existed in the construction of these ancient dwellings. They were not painted but looked very old and well-seasoned. The walls of the house were quite thick made with large blocks of coral which probably helped keep the rooms cool as well as providing the necessary structure to support the palm tree beams. They also added a rustic charm to the house, a time-honoured tribute to the local building techniques. As you observed the small windows on the ground floor you pondered their significance. Perhaps they were a later addition. They seemed to symbolize a careful balance between allowing air to circulate and to provide privacy and security. There weren't that many of them and what windows did exist ensured the sanctity of the home keeping it secluded from the outside world while also acting as a safeguard against potential intruders. The thick walls seemingly standing guard, emphasised the importance of family, community, and protection—values that had endured through generations.

Outside of the house in the allies children played and the fishermen mended their nets. It was just a normal, simple and uncomplicated life. Lots of trading families lived in Shangani, and I would imagine that in Somali terms it was a relatively middle-class and affluent area where multigenerational families lived together, supporting one another, and houses passed from generation to generation. It was a scene that painted a picture of a simple and contented life, where the joys of childhood and the livelihood of fishermen coexisted harmoniously.

I often wonder what happened to Zainab and her family and presume that with the Civil War, they left Somalia and sought refuge either in Kenya or possibly in Pakistan. Staying would have been unthinkable. The reality of the situation makes it difficult to know for certain.

In this very old and traditional neighbourhood the Women's Handicraft Centre, run by a compassionate Danish lady, Brenda Peterson, stood as a beacon of hope and empowerment for the women of Shangani. This was ostensibly a place to teach women new skills such as fabric making, tie-dye and dressmaking, but it also gave women independence and an opportunity to work for themselves. Brenda was a friend of my parents, and my Dad was happily press-ganged into taking photographs at the centre and their work.

The Women's Handicraft Centre in Shangani truly stood as a beacon of hope and progress; it was truly inspiring in an environment that was very male-dominated and where women had little freedom. One sad fact at that was that Female Genital Mutilation (FMG) was the norm, and consequently, infant death at childbirth at that time was close to 60%. In fairness to the authorities this was an acknowledged problem and again where the state collided with faith and local traditions. The fact that the centre provided women with new skills and opportunities to generate income was not just a matter of economic empowerment but also a path towards breaking the chains of oppressive traditions.

The work produced at the centre was awe-inspiring. As a result of the work at the centre the women would sell their products and generate an income. The work produced by these women was a testament to their creativity and resilience. The patterns, colours, and dresses they crafted were a unique reflection of their culture and artistic expression. The centre became a hub of inspiration and a symbol of female independence in the heart of Shangani offering a stark contrast to the prevailing gender norms of the time. It was a valuable centre of creativity and female independence and all in Shangani! It represented a small but significant step towards challenging oppressive practices and creating spaces where women could thrive, not just as artisans but as empowered individuals.

Merchant's house, Shangani

Masjid Abdulaziz, Mogadishu

Shangani building looking out to sea

Somali Women's Handicraft Centre

Chapter 11 - Mogadishu New

Connecting the old parts of the city are relatively modern and planned remnants of the Italian colonial era that follow a grid structure with long colonnades and tree-lined avenues, creating a captivating blend of architectural styles and historical influences. In the centre of the city, you have two key squares, Piazza Solidarity Africana and Piazza Liberta, joined by the main drag, the Corso Somalia. Crisscrossing the Corso Somalia are the Corso Primo Luglio as well as other smaller roads named after other towns and cities across Somalia.

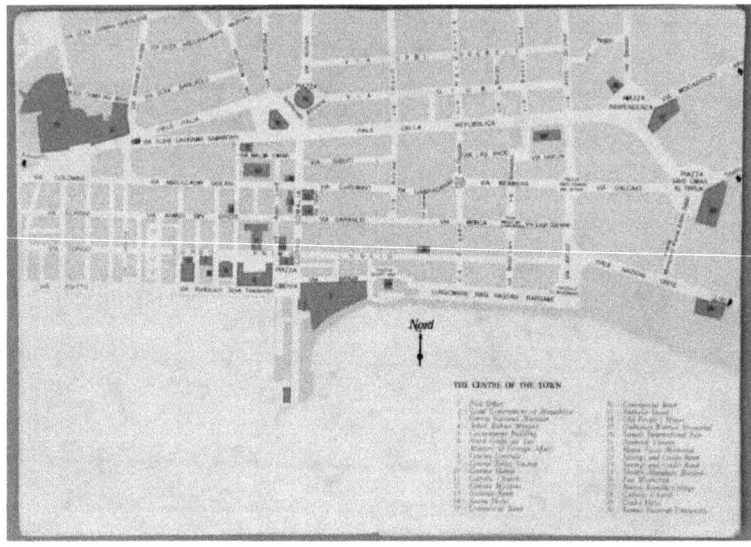

The Italianate cathedral, a testament to the colonial period, proudly stands on Corso Primo Luglio, just a stone's throw from Piazza Liberta. Its architectural design reminiscent of iconic buildings in Rome and Milan, reflects the influence and familiarity that the Italian colonial officers would have experienced during their occupation, and I am sure the Italian officers would have felt very at home here during their period of colonial occupation.

Mogadishu Cathedral

Mogadishu Cathedral, known as the *Cattedrale di Mogadiscio*, was built in 1928 by order of Cesare Maria De Vecchi, governor of Italian Somaliland, who promoted Christianity among the Somali people. The cathedral's construction took six years to complete, and it became a prominent landmark in the city. It was constructed in a Norman Gothic style, based on the Cathedral of Cefalù in Sicily. The choice of this architectural style is intriguing, as the Cathedral of Cefalù was itself built to commemorate the Christian reconquest of Sicily from the Arabs in the 10th century. This decision might have been an intentional effort by the Italian colonial authorities to assert Christian dominance in Mogadishu.

The cathedral was designed by architect Antonio Vandone and built in Norman Gothic style. As per traditional Italianate design the floor plan of the structure was that of a Latin cross with three naves separated by piers with pointed arches. The cathedral's most distinctive feature was its two towering spires, reaching an impressive height of 37.5 meters making it a prominent element of the city's skyline. Initially the cathedral was entrusted to the Consolata missionaries and then subsequently by the Franciscan monks. The cathedral had a regular mass, and I recall the strong scent of incense.

I fondly remember wondering in the square in front of the cathedral just before sunset. Very much like Italian towns and cities the *piazza* is the heart of the urban community and a place to watch life pass around you. It was no different here at the cathedral *piazza*.

Sadly, the cathedral hit the news in 1989 and became a source of controversy and tension in later years. Prior to the outbreak of the Civil War, a few years later, armed insurgents stormed the building whilst the last Bishop of Mogadishu, Father Salvatore Colombo were celebrating mass. Shockingly they shot him dead during the service causing immense grief and outrage within the local Christian community and beyond. Needless to say, there was much controversy surrounding the Bishop's murder and despite calls for an investigation at the time the case remains unsolved. The brutal and brazen attack on a religious leader during a sacred ceremony shocked the nation, Christians and moderate Muslims alike, and highlighted the rising tensions between religious groups.

The circumstances surrounding Bishop Colombo's murder were highly contentious and multiple theories emerged as to who was behind the heinous act. President Siad Barre, who was in power at the time, quickly blamed the assassination on Islamist militants and offered a reward for their capture. However, there has been some speculation that there might be more complex and political motivations behind the killing. Some believed that Siad Barre may have ordered the execution himself for several reasons. Firstly, Bishop Colombo was known to be an outspoken critic of the President and his regime, which could have made him a target. Secondly, the Bishop had helped a clan in purchasing land, which was out of favour with the President, potentially leading to further animosity between the two parties. Lastly, there were suggestions that the murder of the Bishop might have been a calculated move to trigger and garner Western military support and aid for Siad Barre's weakening and ailing government. Whatever the true reason for the Bishop's death it marked a significant turning point in Muslim and Christian relations due to the crackdown that followed. The government intensified its repression of religious groups and any perceived challenges to its authority. This led to further tensions between different religious and ethnic communities, exacerbating the underlying issues that eventually contributed to the outbreak of the Somali Civil War in the early 1990s.

As things began to deteriorate following the death of Bishop Salvatore Colombo and the subsequent outbreak of the Somali Civil War in the early 1990s, the cathedral was no longer regularly used and by late 2008 much of the building was destroyed. The cathedral, once a symbol of religious unity and architectural beauty, fell victim to the violence and destruction that engulfed the city during the conflict. As armed groups and militias fought for control of the city, many buildings, including places of worship, were targeted and damaged. The once-grand Mogadishu Cathedral suffered greatly during this period. By the late 2000s, much of the building had been destroyed leaving only a shell of its former self with no roof.

The diocese inspected the site in April 2013 and announced plans to rebuild the cathedral with hopes of restoring the symbol of peace and unity that it once represented. However, the realities of ongoing conflict, political instability, and economic challenges in Somalia have hampered progress on the reconstruction. Rebuilding the cathedral would require significant resources, expertise, and a stable environment, all of which have been difficult to achieve amidst the continuing turmoil in the country.

The National Museum of Somalia

The National Museum of Somalia (in Somali Matxafka Qarankais and Italian Museo Nazionale della Somalia) was established in 1933 by the Italian colonial authorities and stood as a significant repository of the country's cultural and historical heritage. It was built on the corniche very close to the lighthouse and the Al Arbuba Hotel in Mogadishu and held a vast collection of artefacts, artworks, and historical photographs, providing invaluable insights into Somalia's diverse past. We were regular visitors to the museum privately and with school, and my Dad was a personal friend of the Museum Director. Dad had been asked by the Minister for Culture to help the museum reorganise its photographic archive. The museum had an extensive photographic collection of images of Somalia taken by the Somali authorities. Every image was on glass and taken in the 1930s. Every plate was duplicated and catalogued, and the duplicates were kept for posterity by the National Museum of Somalia, the Museum of Mankind in London, and my Dad himself.

However, the tragic episode of destroying the glass plates that documented various clan and sub-clan identities reveals a darker chapter in Somalia's history. Under the rule of President Siad Barre, the concept of clannism was viewed as a potential threat to the unity and stability of the nation. As a result, the President's Office ordered the eradication of any record of clannism leading to the destruction of these invaluable historical images and records. The destruction of historical artefacts and records is a devastating blow to any society.

The museum was over several floors. The multi-floor layout offered visitors a comprehensive journey through the country's rich history and cultural heritage. On the ground floor, visitors were treated to captivating archaeological and ethnographic exhibitions that showcased artefacts and objects from ancient civilizations, as well as traditional items representing the diverse cultures and customs of different Somali communities. I do recall going on to the roof of the museum, from which you had a good vantage point and could see all around the Liido north. The roof's panoramic view offered a striking contrast between the historic exhibits inside the museum and the modern urban landscape beyond its walls.

Moving up to the first floor, the museum showcased exhibitions that delved into Somalia's struggle for independence and its resistance against colonial rule. This section highlighted the resilience and courage of the Somali people who fought to regain their sovereignty and preserve their cultural identity.

The second floor focused on military history, providing insights into the country's military past and significant events related to warfare and defence. This section likely shed light on Somalia's encounters with various external powers and internal conflicts that have shaped its history.

The museum similarly shut down in 1991, and the building was subsequently destroyed, which was indeed a devastating blow to the preservation of the country's cultural heritage. The outbreak of the Civil War and the subsequent political instability resulted in widespread violence and looting with many historical and archaeological sites falling victim to the chaos. The museum building itself was not spared from the destruction that swept through the city of Mogadishu. During the years of turmoil and the rise of the Islamist insurgency there were significant concerns about the safety and preservation of Somalia's historical artefacts and archives. Many feared that valuable cultural treasures were lost forever adding to the tragedy of the conflict.

However, in September 2019 the museum was rebuilt and reopened, representing a hopeful step toward rebuilding the country's cultural institutions. The restoration of the museum signifies a commitment to preserving Somalia's rich history and promoting cultural understanding. It houses a curated collection of important historical artefacts that have been salvaged and recovered. This includes objects that provide insights into ancient civilizations, traditional cultures, and the struggles for independence and resistance against colonial rule. However, I fear much was destroyed in the Civil War and the Islamist insurgency that followed. 'Hindsight is a beautiful thing', but it is comforting to know that the Museum of Mankind still holds the duplicates of Somalia's photographic collection. These images are valuable not only for their historical content but also as a testament to Somalia's rich cultural diversity and identity. The duplicates serve as a valuable resource for researchers, historians, and Somalis seeking to reconnect with their heritage and history.

Villa Somalia

Villa Somalia, which was originally called Villa del Viceré when inaugurated in October 1936, served as home to the Italian governors. The building was constructed on high ground overlooking the city of Mogadishu and the Indian Ocean and is a significant historical landmark in Mogadishu, reflecting the city's colonial past and its transition to an independent nation. The building was initially simple and square shaped with a tiled roof and then was further developed with a more austere and grand Art Deco edifice similar to other Italianate architecture in the city. Following independence, the building passed from the Italian governorate to become the presidential palace. Villa Somalia became the official residence of the President of Somalia, symbolizing the country's newfound sovereignty and independence. Around this area were the residences of a number of ambassadors, including the British Ambassador's residence. Over the years, the area surrounding Villa Somalia became an important diplomatic quarter, housing the residences of various ambassadors, including the British Ambassador's residence. This proximity to diplomatic missions further emphasized the villa's significance in the realm of international relations.

Throughout its existence, Villa Somalia has witnessed numerous historical events, political changes, and significant moments in Somali history. As the official residence of the President it has hosted numerous state functions, meetings with foreign dignitaries, and official ceremonies, making it a focal point for the country's political life. However, like many buildings in Mogadishu, Villa Somalia also bore the scars of the Civil War and the subsequent unrest that gripped the nation. During the prolonged conflict the palace suffered damage and underwent periods of instability.

Nonetheless, it remained a symbol of national identity and resilience, and efforts have been made to restore and preserve its historical significance.

I had the opportunity of visiting Villa Somalia only on one occasion, but it was memorable. It was done in relative secrecy as we were driven up to the palace for a private audience with HRH Princess Anne, who was in Somalia on a visit to a Save The Children refugee camp on the Somalia border near the Ogaden. Ethiopia was in the grip of another terrible famine on account of the continued failing Marxist economic policies of the Derg regime. The Princess had literally just stepped off her plane and was exhausted. Despite being tired she graciously made polite conversation with my family on the steps leading up to her room. She was solely accompanied by her bodyguard. Princess Anne's visit to Somalia, particularly to the Save The Children refugee camp near the Somalia-Ethiopia border, demonstrated her commitment to humanitarian causes and her concern for those affected by the famine. The famine in Ethiopia had captured the world's attention and led to widespread humanitarian efforts to provide aid and relief to the suffering population.

What I remember of the meeting and the palace was the plush dark blue thick carpet, which reflected the elegance and grandeur of the palace - a stark contrast to the difficult conditions that many people were facing in the region due to the famine. I understand that the Princess did not really want to stay at the palace at all and wanted to fly directly to the refugee camp but she was politically obligated to pass by the President on her way. Not to have stayed would have caused immense offence and setback for many years the then warming of diplomatic relations. Princess Anne's presence at the presidential palace symbolized a connection between the two nations and emphasised the significance of her visit to the refugee camp. However, her genuine concern for the refugee crisis and her humanitarian efforts made the visit much more than just a diplomatic formality. It demonstrated her personal commitment to alleviating suffering and supporting vulnerable populations, as she continues to demonstrate today.

Statue of Sayyid Mohammed Abdullah Hassan

Another notable and significant landmark is the statue of Sayyid Mohammed Abdullah Hassan on *Piazza Solidarieta Africana*. Sayyid Mohammed Abdullah Hassan, also known as the "Mad Mullah," was a prominent leader and nationalist figure who led the Dervish movement in the early 20th century. The Dervish movement sought to unite Somali clans and resist foreign colonial powers, particularly the British and Italians. Sayyid Hassan's vision of a united Somalia resonated with President Siad Barre's ideology of Pan-Somalism, which aimed to unite all Somali-speaking people in the Horn of Africa, including those living in neighbouring countries.

Hassan was an icon of not only Pan-Somalism - a notion very popular with President Siad Barre - but a Pan-African who represented the liberation of African nations from foreign rule and colonization. Close to the Mogadishu Central Mosque, the statue was built of Hassan on his horse Hiin-Faniin and was a Socialist representation of Somalia's liberation from Italian rule and a united Somalia. It stood as a symbol of Somali pride and resistance against foreign rule. The location of the statue, near the Mogadishu Central Mosque, added to its significance, as it reflected the intersection of religion, culture, and national identity.

I understand that during the Civil War, the statue was torn down and the metal was sold for scrap, leaving the damaged foundation. Fortunately, in October 2019, a new statue was restored and unveiled on Piazza Solidarieta Africana by the then-president of Somalia. This restoration marked an important moment in Somalia's efforts to reclaim its cultural heritage and preserve its history. The re-erection of the statue demonstrated the nation's determination to rebuild and unite after years of conflict.

The Bakaara Market

The Bakaara or Bakaaraha market is the main market in Mogadishu and was so in 1983. The Bakaara market is an open market along a long street and was created by then-President Siad Barre in 1972. It wasn't particularly wide, and at the time, each shop and stall had a canvas canopy to provide shade. Bakaara comes from the Somali word *baqaar*, meaning silo or grain storage, no doubt on account of the maize, wheat and sorghum historically sold here. Over time, the market has evolved to accommodate a diverse range of goods and services, becoming a bustling centre of commerce for both locals and traders from various regions.

In 1983, the market was a vibrant and bustling place, with stalls and shops lining the long street. The canvas canopies provided essential shade for both the vendors and customers in the warm Somali climate. Each stall offered essentially local produce - banana, mango, guava and grapefruit. I don't recall buying very much from the market other than grapefruit. Given their abundance locally, we would juice them at home and add to our tasteless desalinated water.

The Bakaara market's significance extends beyond its role as a commercial space. It also represents a central meeting point for people from different walks of life, fostering a sense of community and social interaction. The market's lively atmosphere and the exchange of goods and cultural practices make it a vital cultural landmark in Mogadishu.

There was a butcher that sold goat, camel, and some beef but not a great deal beyond that. What I do remember very clearly are the mountains of discarded animal offal and bones. It was quite a sight and quite a smell! For a predominantly pastoralist society like Somalia, where livestock plays a crucial role in their culture and economy, the availability of fresh meat is of utmost importance. The butcher stalls were a vital part of the market, catering to the locals' dietary preferences and providing a source of sustenance and income for both traders and customers.

However, what stood out prominently in the market were the mountains of discarded animal offal and bones. In traditional Somali culture, almost every part of the slaughtered animals is utilized, and nothing goes to waste. The edible parts are sold, consumed, and enjoyed by the locals, while the remaining parts are discarded in piles. The sight and smell of the offal and bones provided a stark reminder of the market's lively trade and the essential role of livestock in the Somali way of life.

At the very start of the market there was also a fishmonger that primarily sold tuna. As previously mentioned, fish was not a prevalent part of the Somali diet given their pastoralist heritage and emphasis on livestock-based food sources. Therefore, the availability of massive tuna at the fishmonger's stall might have been an unusual sight for many locals. The tuna was absolutely massive and around 80 cm in length. The tuna meat was a deep bloody red, which would have been an eye-catching contrast to the more familiar red meat of the other butcher stalls.

The Battle of Mogadishu, famously depicted in the film *"Black Hawk Down"*, occurred on the 3rd and 4th of October 1993, during the United Nations-sanctioned operation to capture Somali warlord Mohamed Farrah Aidid. The mission involved US Army Rangers and Delta Force soldiers, along with United Nations peacekeeping forces. Bakaara market was one of the key areas where the intense urban combat took place.

During the operation, two US Army Black Hawk helicopters were shot down by rocket-propelled grenades in the vicinity of Bakaara market. This event triggered a prolonged and fierce firefight that lasted throughout the day and into the evening of the 4th of October. The battle was marked by heavy casualties on both sides, with many US soldiers wounded or killed, and it remains one of the most significant and intense military engagements in recent history.

Since the Battle of Mogadishu, the Bakaara market has continued to face challenges, including attacks by the extremist group Al-Shabaab. As a highly populated and central location in Mogadishu, the market has been a target for terrorist activities. Al-Shabaab, an Islamist militant group with a strong presence in Somalia, has carried out numerous attacks on civilian areas, including markets like Bakaara.

Bakaara market since then hasn't really been able to keep out of the limelight and has been the location of a number of Al Shabaab attacks and fires. Indeed in 2011 the African Union Mission to Somalia and the Transitional Federal Government launched an offensive to clear the market of Al Shabaab. There are several books that cover the influence of Al Shabaab that can be found in the bibliography that perhaps explains why the market in the centre of Mogadishu is such a magnet for terror. The security situation in Mogadishu has remained fragile and the market has experienced subsequent attacks and fires over the years. Bakaara market's history is deeply intertwined with the socio-political landscape of Somalia, reflecting the challenges and complexities of the country's prolonged conflict and its struggle to establish stability and security. Despite the hardships, the market continues to play a vital role in the daily lives of many Somalis, serving as a major trading hub and a place of commerce and community.

***

As a footnote, my wife and I recently spent a week in the alluring city of Florence, or Firenze as it is known in Italy, steeped in profound history and with architectural beauty.

One evening, we ventured from our cool top-floor snug apartment nestled in the historical heart of the city, situated tantalisingly close to the breath-taking Duomo, and wandered northeast towards a nearby suburb. As we strolled through the maze of narrow cobblestone streets lined with centuries-old buildings, we entered a modern and more architecturally open suburb. I couldn't help but feel a surge of familiarity wash over me. The whole scene seemed to echo a past experience - as we would turn onto the Corso Somalia, heading north past the old lighthouse, and then turn left into the square in front of the cathedral.

A captivating energy permeated the open areas close to a church where locals were engrossed in casual banter with friends, each absorbed in catching up on the day's events. The backdrop of the setting sun casting long, mellow shadows, and the invigorating cool of the early evening further amplified the atmosphere. The interactions resonated with the warmth and rhythm of humanity, effortlessly blending the old with the new, creating a vivid tapestry of life that harked back to my memories of Mogadishu.

The architecture, while bearing the imprint of a shared historical epoch, is where Florence and Mogadishu diverge strikingly. Both cities bear architectural imprints of the 13th century, yet they offer starkly different visual narratives. Florence, famous for its Renaissance-inspired architecture, speaks of an era of humanistic revival, a blend of innovation and a return to classical architectural forms.

On the other hand, old Mogadishu is a testament to East African Islamic architectural influences, particularly its many mosques, radiating an adherence to intricate geometric patterns and designs.

The difference in these architectural styles tells a tale of two cultures, two histories, and two identities coalescing, creating a contrasting yet fascinating backdrop.

One example in Florence that stood out to me and could well have been a building in new Mogadishu was the work of architect Rodolfo Sabatini, the *Casa del Mutilato*. Every day, I would find myself in the shadow of this monolithic edifice, patiently awaiting my wife as she finished her day on an art course at the Apollon Art School situated in the Piazza Brunelleschi.

Despite its modernist appeal, the architecture of the Casa del Mutilato is rooted in fascism, explicitly manifesting itself in its design. Its form and presence are intended to project an unyielding sense of power, statehood, and control. This striking piece of architecture served as a stark contrast to the Renaissance buildings of Florence.

That is exactly what I fondly remember from Mogadishu: a contrast in architectural styles from different eras that somehow just naturally fit together.

Chapter 12 - Living on the Afgooye Road

Our family home was one of four villas built at kilometre 20 on the Afgooye Road as the road reaches its highest point coming out of Mogadishu. The villa was a large open-plan construction set on about a quarter of an acre of land. The double gate at the entrance provided both security and privacy, setting the property apart from the main road and ensuring a sense of seclusion within the surrounding landscape. A concrete drive led into the property and continued to the top left corner where there was an open high height and open double garage. Dad was passionate about his Land Rover as it was one of the first V8 long wheelbase models. The Land Rover V8 long-wheelbase model was a versatile and rugged vehicle well-suited for navigating the challenging terrain of the region. Soon after arrival he swapped the standard Land Rover-supplied tyres for a set of sand tyres leaving the standard tyres stacked neatly in the corner of his garage. The desert paths to the south of Jazeerah, known for their soft and shifting sands, posed a challenge for many vehicles. These tyres were formidable and enabled him to quite simply float over the sand of the desert paths to the south of Jazeerah, whilst many would just get stuck. However, they certainly weren't road tyres and we could generally hear him from about half a kilometre away as he approached the house.

During this time Somalia was experiencing significant political and social changes. The early 1980s were marked by the authoritarian rule of President Siad Barre, who sought to centralise power and implement socialist policies. As the country faced internal tensions and regional conflicts, our family's peaceful oasis provided a safe haven from the uncertainties of the outside world.

The concrete drive on entry also extended to the right of the property and, from there wrapped around the front of the house and connected directly to the veranda. Around the villa was compacted sand. The combination of concrete and compacted sand on the driveways and pathways was well-suited for the local climate and provided a clean and orderly look to the property. The sand pathways likely allowed for proper drainage during the rainy season preventing water from pooling and causing damage.

The property boundary was square shaped with the concrete driveway an L shape in the bottom left of the square. Around the perimeter were East African flame trees of about 5 to 6 metres in height and their branches and foliage connected providing considerable shade. These trees are known for their vibrant red flowers and dense foliage making them popular for landscaping purposes in the city. The use of decorative bricks around the veranda wall added a touch of elegance to the property's design. The cool shade provided by the trees would have been especially appreciated during the hot and sunny days making the veranda and outdoor spaces ideal for relaxation and gatherings. This type of architectural detailing was common in many homes and buildings across Somalia and East Africa, reflecting a blend of traditional and modern influences.

In the top right-hand corner of the property was the maid's toilet and a storage room. The security measures were typical features in many properties in Somalia and other parts of the region. The perimeter wall was about 2 metres high and lined atop with large shards of broken glass bottles. These measures were employed to deter potential intruders and protect the privacy of the residents. During that time security was an important consideration given the political and social complexities of the region. In other words, gaining access would be challenging and painful.

Walking up the main set of stairs at the front, you access a very large open veranda which, aside from the entrance, was surrounded on its open sides by a wall of decorative bricks and approximately 1.5 metres high. The veranda with its decorative wall and open sides would have been a perfect spot for family gatherings, entertaining guests, or simply enjoying the breeze and view of the surrounding landscape. It also led to the main entrance to the house.

Entering the house was a large, long hallway that opened to the left to a very large open-plan lounge and dining room. To the right of the hallway were the bedrooms and family bathroom. The large open-plan lounge and dining room would have been a central gathering area for family and guests providing ample space for socialising, dining, and relaxation. The open design likely allowed for good ventilation, which would have been appreciated in the warm climate of Somalia. There were three bedrooms in total and one family-sized bathroom. From the dining room, in the top left corner of the building, was a door that led into the kitchen, which provided privacy and separation from the communal areas of the house. The kitchen wasn't particularly large and to the back of the kitchen was a storage room.

Prior to being posted to Somalia, my parents had to purchase considerable provisions given the relative food scarcity and challenging conditions due to various factors, including political instability, economic difficulties, and droughts in the country. This effectively meant purchasing two years' worth of dried and tinned food supplies. We had considerable amounts of dried pasta and tinned tomatoes!! These were all stored either in the storeroom off the kitchen or in the third bedroom. For all intents and purposes, we were completely self-sufficient from a food perspective.

The building's height was about 3.5 metres, and it had a tarred flat roof. On the roof surrounding the square building was a wall of about 1 metre in height. Also on the roof in the top right corner was a freshwater tank, considering the scarcity of clean water in the region. Each month a water truck would turn up and hoses were slung over our wall at the side and onto the roof and the water tank was refilled. The water came from Mogadishu's desalination plant. Given the age of the truck and the water tank it was unsafe to drink the water straight from the tap. We would have a regular weekly process of boiling water and filling water bottles and large containers with cooked boiled water. Boiling the water and storing it in bottles was a necessary step to make sure it was safe for consumption. The bottles were then placed in the fridge.

Somalia's hot climate, especially during the height of summer, would have necessitated a regular and increased intake of water to prevent heat exhaustion and dehydration. Needless to say, the water tasted pretty unpleasant and we eventually resorted to adding freshly squeezed grapefruit juice to the water just to make it taste a little bit better. Given the temperatures we also had to maintain our water intake. Ensuring proper hydration was essential to cope with the heat and maintain good health in the challenging environment. I was on several occasions ill in bed for days with heat exhaustion and dehydration on account of simply not consuming enough water. Mum had brought out from the UK an electric juicer and we could get grapefruit from the Bakaara market inexpensively and make the juice to help flavour our water. We had a production line going on a regular basis.

Somalia is the only place I have ever experienced sunstroke or heat exhaustion and on a number of occasions, and that is despite having lived and travelled in many equally hot countries. The experience of sunstroke in Somalia was particularly intense which is not surprising given that Mogadishu is 400 kilometres from the Equator. Generally, I had been outside in the sun, no doubt without a hat, for an extended period of time.

The first symptoms I experienced were dizziness and confusion. I recall on one occasion standing up at lunch from the dining room table and being completely delirious babbling to my parents and then promptly throwing up everywhere much to everyone's alarm and consternation. It was entirely an automatic response over which I pretty well had no rational control. I recall subsequently resting initially with an absolutely throbbing headache and then sleeping for hours in a dark air-conditioned room. Occasionally I would experience stomach cramps, but it was the headaches that were unbearable. Mum would apply a cold compress to try and keep my temperature down.

This would literally last for days. Mum would ensure that I was hydrated, and I took paracetamol to manage the general pain and headaches. I would feel exhausted for what felt like an eternity. It was only on about day three that I would begin to start to feel normal again and able to eat anything. I had sunstroke on several occasions in Somalia but have never experienced anything like them since. They were truly unbearable.

The buildings were cooled by overhead fans and also each bedroom had air conditioning creating a more comfortable living space. The fans and air conditioning units are particularly appreciated during the hot and humid summer months when temperatures could become quite intense. As we had been cross posted from Saudi Arabia, my parents had also brought with them uprights fans also, which in the height of the summer heat, came into their own, helping to manage the heat effectively.

The property was furnished with standard-issue Foreign Office furniture, which was complimented by soft furnishings and rugs that my parents had purchased in Saudi Arabia. Indeed, one of the large rugs measuring 2 metres by 3 metres would subsequently fill the floor of my school study when we left Somalia and I went to boarding school.

The use of standard-issue Foreign Office furniture in the property reflects the practicality and efficiency required for official postings. While it may not have been aesthetically exciting, it served its purpose well, offering functional and durable furnishings suitable for diplomatic residences around the world. The addition of soft furnishings and rugs purchased in Saudi Arabia added a touch of comfort and personalisation to the living space making it feel more like home.

I do recall that the lounge and dining room open plan area was rather dark due to the heavy metallic fly netting in the outside of the windows and, of course, the shutters. The objective was to keep the property as cool as possible and to combat the hot climate. Somalia's tropical climate, with high temperatures and abundant sunshine, necessitated these protective measures to shield the interior from direct sunlight and heat. I should point out that having the air conditioning on full-time wasn't helpful either, as constantly coming in and out of the air conditioning from the heat outside was a recipe for disaster and would make you sick. Finding the right balance between using air conditioning and adapting to the natural environment was crucial for maintaining comfort and health.

We were lucky enough to have both a Betamax and a VHS video player and television, which was novel, and Dad had an arrangement with a neighbour in the UK to record British TV programmes such as Faulty Towers, Dad's Army, and Top of the Pops. There was also a weekly news round-up programme. The tapes would appear roughly every two to three weeks in the Diplomatic Bag from the UK. The availability of entertainment provided a sense of connection to home and offered a welcome respite from the challenges of living in a foreign country with limited access to familiar media.

In addition, Dad, in his capacity as Cultural Attaché, also had films and news reels sent out to the UK ostensibly to put on for the locals! Via this route we got the latest blockbuster films. We also got all the news reels covering at the time the then all important Falklands War, which, without from the BBC World Service and an FCO news service we would have been completely cut off from. These news reels and radio broadcasts were critical to staying up to date on international affairs.

Mum and Dad would organise film supper evenings and friends from foreign embassies would be invited over to watch a film. This was a brilliant way to foster a sense of community among the expatriate community. It offered a opportunity for people to come together and enjoy popular films and just have a good time making the best use of the resources available.

Typically, a dinner course would be served between reels. Looking back now these were probably way ahead of their time, and the friends coming over ordinarily had access to nothing unless they were able to watch the films shown at the America Embassy swimming pool and recreation area.

We would also have excellent barbecues. The barbecues and gatherings on the veranda with friends were a popular and social way of enjoying meals and bringing people together for a relaxed and enjoyable time.

Dad had his iron plate barbecue shipped from Australia to Saudi Arabia to Somalia and, using breeze blocks, had built a barbecue at the front of the house on a piece of dirt to the side. It served as a clever and practical way to accommodate our family's desire for outdoor cooking and socializing with friends. When it wasn't humid and the evenings were cool, we would often have a barbecue with friends and eat out on the veranda. The barbecues on the veranda, especially during cooler evenings, provided a pleasant atmosphere for gatherings and fostered a sense of community with friends and neighbours. Again the food would be basic and primarily fish or whatever meat my parents could get hold of. My parents also had a well-stocked bar with beer and spirits courtesy of the

British Army NAAFI in Nairobi. We also had access to a duty-free catalogue service and goods were also shipped that way to post.

My parents have never been particularly into retaining house servants and preferred their privacy. However, there was an expectation locally that my parents employ staff and contribute to the local economy. We had a gatekeeper or '*boab*' called Adow and a housemaid called Dofar.

Adow was an older guy and was key to ensuring the property was secure. I do remember accompanying my Dad to take Adow to the local hospital as his wife had sadly miscarried. I can recall him being naturally so devasted and upset and my Dad looked after him like a brother. Whilst Adow was technically an employee there was a closeness between us as a family and him.

We also had the dog for protection, and despite how dogs are perceived in Muslim society the dog got on remarkably well with Adow. The only security issue we had was youths throwing stones at our metal gate, especially during times of political and social unrest. Unfortunately, this became a regular occurrence and so on a couple of occasions, the gate was opened and the dog was released to chase them off. We didn't have to do this very often and nobody was hurt. It was simply used as an effective deterrent to dissuade the youths from stoning the property. I am sure they also knew about the dog and were trying to purely antagonise it.

Dofar's role as a housemaid highlights the complexities of hiring local staff overseas. Dofar was a young girl of eighteen years of age from the nearby village of Afgooye. Each day she would catch the bus to and from our house. My Mum naturally mothered her, and in all honesty, she wasn't really much of a housemaid. She wasn't very good in the kitchen and she didn't really like cleaning or ironing. I know my Mum used to get frustrated with her for essentially not doing very much. She also had a habit of not having particularly good food hygiene in the kitchen, which was problematic in a country where picking up a bug was commonplace. Mum was a kind lady and persevered. I recall that whenever Dofar accidentally broke something like a glass, she was immediately in a panic and started crying, "*Mrs Tunnicliffe*". Being youngsters, we had a nickname for her, which wasn't particularly flattering: do-farts! Thinking about it now, she wasn't much older than me in reality and probably liked being mothered by my Mum.

So how does a youngster entertain themselves in such a location? The trees at the back of the property were much higher than the flame trees that surrounded it. They offered a perfect playground for exploration and imaginative play. Climbing trees and playing among the foliage would have been adventurous and thrilling for a young child, offering a sense of freedom and escape from the confines of the house. On one occasion, I took the hand-winch off the front of my Dad's Land Rover and hooked it up high in one tree and then extended the cable across the garden to another tree and I created a "death slide". It was absolutely lethal and soon the novelty wore off!

I did also, as any young lad would, climb in the flame trees to the side of the property, and on one occasion ended up in a pile on the dirt floor. It's a miracle that I didn't break any bones! African bees loved building their nests in these trees and they would bite into the branches and hollow out the softwood core, no doubt devouring the sugars in the softer sweet wood. The net effect was to make the branch structurally weak and hence with me applying my weight, it just snapped like a match. During that time the country faced political unrest and civil conflict, and there were limited options for traditional entertainment or recreational activities. As a result, expatriate families had to find ways to make the most of their surroundings and create their own fun and games.

Living in Mogadishu during the 1980s provided an opportunity to experience a unique blend of wildlife and diplomatic life. There wasn't much in the way of wildlife in the garden aside from African bees, geckos, cockroaches and stink ants. The stink ants were about an inch long and called stink ants because the moment you stepped on one it would release a pretty obnoxious smell clearly designed to deter a predator. In terms of common birds we had two species: The first was the weaver bird which was skilled nest builder. They had found a welcoming habitat in the flame trees that provided shelter and safety for their nests. These charismatic birds added colour and activity to the garden with their bustling nest-building activities. The other was a hoopoe bird. A rather majestic bird that would fly into the garden and proudly display its plume. Interestingly today, the Somali National Intelligence Service (NIS) emblem is a hoopoe and their officers are affectionately known as hoopoes. We did have some pretty dangerous animals on occasion but fortunately, very rarely. We had scorpions and small vipers. The vipers were about 40 cm in length and would timidly hide on the trunk of the flame trees.

Our house was one of four villas and all were exactly identical and on the same size plot. The close-knit community of diplomatic families formed a unique support network. One property was home to someone that worked for the British Council, another to someone that worked for the Overseas Development Agency (ODA) and the other to a management officer that worked in the Embassy with my Dad. There were no other children in the post. The Ambassador, Head Chancery and the Ambassador's PA all lived in downtown Mogadishu relatively close to Villa Somalia, the Presidential Palace. The embassy staff were all connected by a CB radio net that my dad had put in place just in case something happened. Somali was a revolutionary state and arguably politically volatile and susceptible to coups.

Our villas were set out on their own and at the crest of a hill about a kilometre from the American School of Mogadishu where we went to school and Mum taught. Being situated on a hilltop with a view of the surroundings provided a sense of seclusion and security for the villas. I often wonder what subsequently happened during and after the Civil War and would imagine that the embassy staff were moved to a safe haven in Nairobi and locals fleeing the fighting in Mogadishu took refuge in the four villas and their grounds. The turbulent political climate in Somalia at that time necessitated such preparedness to address potential emergencies. The villas, once homes to diplomatic families, might have provided refuge to locals fleeing the fighting in the surrounding area, seeking safety and shelter amid the chaos of war.

Living in a location that was relatively isolated and in the middle of nowhere had its pros and cons. On the one hand, it provided a sense of security and privacy, which was especially important in a country like

Somalia, with its political instability and potential security risks. The proximity to the airport and the US embassy compound, along with the presence of the well-armed US Marines Corp added an extra layer of protection and reassurance for the diplomatic community.

It goes without saying that whilst our arrival in Mogadishu was certainly a shock, we made the very best of it we could. Dad built a dark room in our bathroom where he would regularly process film and make prints. It's worth pointing out that many of his black-and-white photographs were processed this way, and if you look closely, you can see that mineral sediments in the water would leave very tiny dots and marks in his images. The unique markings left by the water's mineral sediments on his black and white photographs became an unintentional but distinctive characteristic of his work adding a touch of authenticity and uniqueness to his images.

However, living in a relatively remote location also meant limited access to everyday amenities and conveniences. What people may not appreciate, and I am sure this was entirely by design; the properties were literally in the middle of nowhere. We didn't live amongst the population at all and, to a degree, were a bit cut off. It wasn't likely we could walk around the corner to a shop. Again I am sure, from a close protection perspective, this was entirely by design. We were situated outside of the city but relatively close to the airport, so it wouldn't be very difficult for us to evacuate if necessary. It wasn't like we had a city to navigate in order to get to the airport, and we were in close proximity to the US embassy compound and the so-called Jolly Green Giant home to at least 30 well-armed US Marines. In addition, the road immediately outside of our house was long enough and wide enough to land a C130 in the event of an emergency evacuation. This demonstrated the seriousness with which the diplomatic community regarded safety and preparedness for any potential emergencies or evacuation scenarios.

Living in a remote location, away from the bustling city certainly had its drawbacks, one of which was limited access to everyday amenities and fresh produce. The only hardship we had to really endure, aside from the real lack of fresh fruit and vegetables such as tomatoes, carrots, apples and the like, was the occasional power cuts and power instability. The country's infrastructure, including its energy grid, was underdeveloped and struggling to meet the increasing demand for electricity. Frequent power outages could be disruptive and sometimes prolonged, affecting daily routines and access to modern conveniences. Dad had a regulator that maintained stable power to devices such as the videotape machine and the open reel stereo and radio. However, we frequently ensured powered cuts for extended periods of time. The challenge was, at the time, that the infrastructure was poor and couldn't cope with the ever-increasing demand for energy.

The presence of the US embassy compound and the well-armed US Marines in close proximity to your residence likely provided a sense of security and reassurance, knowing that help and support were nearby if needed. The location of our house, with its proximity to the airport and the availability of an emergency landing strip, further emphasized the importance of preparedness and safety for the diplomatic community.

On the whole, living in Mogadishu was an adventure, and for years afterwards, I would do nothing but talk about our time there and experiences which perhaps explains my nickname from some friends at university: As-Somaal or the Somali. Whilst an adventure, the reader should not underestimate the serious challenges associated with living in this environment.

However, it's essential not to overlook the serious health risks and dangers that exist in the environment. I will never forget one of Dad's ODA colleagues who had been working on a farming project in the vicinity of the River Shabelle. He had inadvertently drank contaminated water, no doubt from the river itself. He ended up with Bilharzia (also known as schistosomiasis), a parasitic disease caused by liver flukes, which highlights the real health hazards that people faced in the region. Bilharzia is transmitted through contaminated water sources, often found in rivers and lakes, and it can lead to severe health complications, including liver and urinary system damage. I remember him clutching it as it was visibly enlarged as he boarded his aircraft to go home to die. The lack of access to safe and clean water made it more challenging to avoid such diseases, and medical facilities might not have been equipped to handle certain conditions, especially in remote areas.

Dad also got seriously ill, contracting both Meningitis and Hepatitis again, no doubt, from a handshake, utensils or some other transfer of infection. This highlights the real health risks and challenges that exist in the country. In environments where healthcare infrastructure may have been limited and public health measures were not as well-established, infections like Meningitis and Hepatitis could spread more easily. The source of infection transmission in such situations could be through everyday interactions. He was so ill that he had to be flown to the hospital in Nairobi leaving us behind in Mogadishu. It was highly likely that whatever he had may have been passed on to us, not that we were tested at the time.

Mogadishu, like many parts of Somalia during that period, faced a high burden of infectious diseases and illnesses due to factors such as lack of clean water, poor sanitation, and limited access to healthcare services. At the time, illness and infection were prevalent everywhere in so many countries, the UK included. They had health programmes set up urgently to train doctors to effectively treat the health challenges faced by the population. I, therefore, always reflected on the start of the Coronavirus in 2020 and how a country like Somalia would cope in the face of a major pandemic and following 30 years of civil war, terrorism and political unrest. The pandemic has put a strain on healthcare systems worldwide, and countries with already fragile infrastructures were particularly vulnerable. The resilience of the Somali people and the warmer climate may have provided some advantages in slowing the spread of the virus, but the overall impact of the pandemic on vulnerable populations cannot be underestimated. Perhaps the only saving grace was the resilience of the Somali people and the survivability of the virus in the heat.

Living and working in Somalia during those times demanded a high level of caution, adaptability, and vigilance. The country's political instability, limited infrastructure, and healthcare challenges were significant concerns for expatriates and locals alike. It also speaks to the resilience and courage of those who chose to work and live in such environments, taking on responsibilities that often had far-reaching impacts on the communities they served.

Chapter 13 - Visitors

The regular pattern of life in Mogadishu followed a particular order that many would find repetitive but for us was very special. With weekends spent at the beach, this leisure time provided our family with a sense of normalcy and relaxation amidst the unique challenges of living in a foreign country and a complex environment. It allowed us to make the most of our time and enjoy the beautiful beaches that Somalia had to offer. These weekend getaways were likely a much-needed break from the daily routine and provided an opportunity for quality family time and socialising with friends. Dad was on duty every other weekend, which meant that when he was on duty he couldn't wander too far from the Embassy. On those days we would perhaps have a barbecue with friends at home and go on an evening drive down the coast. However, when he wasn't rostered we would head to the beach and camp out overnight. As previously mentioned, we were extremely lucky and the beaches in Somalia truly rival any others in the Indian Ocean.

The beaches of Somalia are renowned for their natural beauty and are indeed among the finest in the Indian Ocean. The coastal regions of the country boast stunning white sandy shores, crystal-clear waters, and a diverse marine ecosystem, making them ideal spots for camping and beach activities. Enjoying these picturesque locations allowed our family to connect with nature and experience the wonders of Somalia's coastal landscape.

This was a regular pattern, and of course during the week Dad was at work at the embassy and Mum and us three children were at school - Mum taught in the preschool. The work at the embassy involved engaging with various officials and stakeholders in Somalia on not just cultural matters but in Dad's other role as Head of the British Council in Somalia, securing places for Somali graduates in British universities. At the same time, the Mum's role in the preschool was key in creating that link and connection with the American community in Somalia with whom we spent a lot of our social time.

The pattern was, on occasion, interrupted by visitors and visiting warships. My parents were always welcoming when visitors came to town and a highlight that was talked about in the weeks that followed.

On one occasion Dad had an ODA ornithologist visit post who was studying migratory birds. The visit became an incident that highlights the sensitive and often paranoid atmosphere of the regime during that time. I recall that we drove down to the main square - Piazza Liberta - to meet him. He had a small portable tape recorder slung over his shoulder. He had been staying at the Croce del Sud Hotel, which was run by the Briatta family from Padua in Italy. On a subsequent evening, this chap, whose name escapes me, had been wandering the square and the quiet streets near his hotel recording the sounds of migratory birds on his specialist recording device. Needless to say, this didn't go down well at all with the authorities and the Somalia National Security Service (NSS) who had been observing his seemingly odd behaviour immediately picked him up and took him to their headquarters. They began interrogating and questioning what on earth he was doing. The fact that the NSS took swift action to investigate the ornithologist's activities underscores the heightened security measures in place and the government's vigilance against any perceived threats, real or imagined. NSS assumed that his portable tape recorder was some form of listening device with the intent of spying. My Dad then received a call from the Ministry of Foreign Affairs to come to the ODA scientist's aid and to explain that he had come to Somalia on legitimate academic business to record migratory birds and not to spy on the President!

The combination of living under a paranoid dictator in a revolutionary state and dealing with the National Security Service (NSS) made it crucial for foreign visitors and diplomats to be cautious in their actions and communications. Such an event may now seem absurd but it was not untypical given the sensitivity of the regime to anything that may be construed as a potential threat to the state and again that is the irony as we look back now that many Somalis will have a perhaps rose-tinted view of Somalia as though prior to the Civil War nothing bad ever happened. The example just demonstrates the paranoia of the regime at this sensitive time.

During this time, Somalia's political landscape was characterized by tension and instability. The government, led by President Siad Barre, was known for its strict control and harsh measures against any form of opposition. The NSS was instrumental in maintaining the regime's grip on power and enforcing its policies. Any individual or incident that raised suspicion could lead to immediate investigation and questioning. In the context of the Civil War and the subsequent collapse of the government, many people might indeed hold a romanticised view of Somalia's pre-war era. However, your personal experiences and the stories from that time provide a more nuanced perspective, shedding light on the challenges and complexities of living under such a regime.

Every now and then we would have visits by the Queen's Messenger from Nairobi. Whilst perhaps not significant, these visits were a welcomed event for the small British diplomatic community in Mogadishu. The Queen's Messenger is a British diplomatic courier responsible for carrying and delivering important and confidential documents, known as the Diplomatic Bag, between British embassies and high commissions around the world and London. They were a lifeline in an environment where we had little interaction with the outside world save for the BBC World Service.

Typically the Queen's Messengers didn't stay and simply flew up from Nairobi, dropped and collected new Diplomatic Bags and then flew straight back. On one notable occasion a Queen's Messenger known to my Dad, did stay for one night and kindly brought with him some supplies from Nairobi, which included fresh fruit and vegetables and some sweets for us. The excitement and gratitude for fresh fruit and vegetables, especially carrots, was enormous. Such basic commodities in Mogadishu during that time were extremely scarce and most of our food was tinned or dried. He was completely taken aback when we ignored the sweets and went straight for the carrots! We were in complete awe.

As Cultural Attaché Dad had a pianist called Richard Deering visit the post for an official cultural tour. It seems quite surreal now but then entirely the norm. The intent was to use these visits to promote cultural exchanges and foster relationships with the local diplomatic and academic community. This celebrated pianist would perform a number of concerts during his visit to Mogadishu at the Ambassador's residence to Somali dignitaries and local diplomats. He also played a concert at the American School where I was a student. It was all very surreal in many respects having a classical pianist perform in a country dealing with conflict and famine but a pleasant interlude. Richard Deering's visit was a cultural highlight and a success that was talked about for weeks afterwards giving Dad much kudos with the boss, Ambassador Michael Purcell.

One of Dad's other duties was 'meeting and greeting' British Warships that paid Mogadishu a port visit. There was no Defence Attaché in post and given his ten-year career in the Merchant Navy at the equivalent rank of Lieutenant-Commander it was entirely appropriate he welcomed the visiting warships. It was politically at a time when President Siad Barre was pivoting away from his allegiance to the Soviet Union and moving slowly towards the US and her allies. There was clearly an uptick in visiting warships from the US and the UK at this time. These visits symbolised the strengthening of ties and cooperation between Somalia and the Western powers during that period and helped bolster Siad Barre.

On one visit we had the Type 42 destroyer HMS Cardiff call and stay in port for around five days. The Falklands War at this point hadn't started but tensions were brewing in the South Atlantic. HMS Cardiff stopped in Mogadishu on its way supposedly home to the UK. Embassy staff and families were invited onboard the ship, and again, we were overwhelmed with the generosity of a well-stocked ship that had just sailed up the east coast of Africa from South Africa. These port visits demonstrated the diplomatic and humanitarian aspects of such naval missions, creating opportunities for relationship building and goodwill between the naval forces and the local government. What we didn't appreciate, perhaps, was that this was the ship's last port of call before Gibraltar, where it would be re-tasked to join Task Force South heading to the South Atlantic as a component of the naval flotilla steaming to the Falklands conflict.

Whilst not a British warship, the visit of the USS Dixie, a US Navy ship equipped with an onboard hospital and dental facilities, provided a valuable opportunity for the British Embassy staff and their families to access medical and dental care in Mogadishu, where such services locally may have been limited or difficult to obtain. The ship's medical facilities offered a range of services, including routine check-ups, treatments, and dental cleanings.

The USS Dixie's port visit to Mogadishu served not only diplomatic but humanitarian purposes providing aid and support to the Somali government and politically demonstrated the US's commitment to humanitarian assistance in the region.

These visitors to Mogadishu added to our experience of living in Somalia. I wouldn't say that our life was monotonous, but the visits naturally broke up our time them, added to our experience and were a point of discussion not only in anticipation and during a visit but often for many weeks after. This was an interesting time in Somalia's history when it was slowly pivoting away from the Soviet East and reengaging with the world outside and importantly culturally reengaging.

Chapter 14 - Farewell

Leaving Somalia was less eventful than our arrival and all seemed to happen in a rush – or you could say, we were now quite familiar with the drill of packing and boarding a plane at any given time. Mum and Dad were keen that we would be back in the UK before the end of the school year In the UK to ensure I secured a new boarding school place before the start of the next academic year. Plans were somewhat scuppered when Dad's replacement resigned on news of his posting to Mogadishu - in those days, you were told where you were posted and didn't really have much choice in the matter. That meant Dad would have to remain on post for a few months on his own until his replacement arrived. That meant we didn't have much of a farewell as a family and any farewell reception was for Dad after we had left.

The family's departure was therefore disjointed given that we were leaving ahead of Dad. He was given time to dispose of our personal effects. The plan was to take as little as possible home. Firstly, it wouldn't be needed and, importantly, we had nowhere to store it at home in the UK! Lastly, Dad would have more room to carry luggage upon his next posting since he'd only bring his belongings. Unlike our move to Somalia, it wasn't clear where Dad would be posted next, and indeed, he wouldn't be posted for another 12 months.

On the day of departure our bags were packed and Dad drove us to the airport accompanied by the embassy fixer. The role of the fixer was to smooth things over with the officials. This was a well-trodden path and as we approached the airport the gate to the left of the terminal building was opened and we drove onto the tarmac right up to the plane. Completely inconceivable today particularly after September 11th. We were given our Somali Airlines boarding cards and our hold luggage, which was then tagged to London, taken directly to the aircraft and loaded into the hold. As was the norm we completely bypassed check-in and walked from the Land Rover directly onto the plane.

In front of us was a gleaming Boeing 707, a four-engined jet, and steps connected the aircraft front and back. The plane could seat more than

180 passengers — a point of wonderment in those years. It was one of three 707s Somali Airlines operated. The airline was the flag carrier of Somalia and offered flights for both domestic and international travellers. The airline had a training partnership with Lufthansa, and invariably, one of the Lufthansa cabin crew trainers, who we knew, greeted us warmly.

Soon after we had climbed the steps we moved down the aisle to find our seats. Dad made sure we were all settled into our seats ready to go and we quickly said our goodbyes. Even though our departure from Somalia was not how we expected it to be, it all happened in a flash – the packing, the change in plans, and now the flight. He gave my Mum a quick cuddle and a kiss, turned and was gone. I don't think it really registered that we wouldn't be seeing him for a while. There were no tears, just a wave, good wishes, some instructions and then the take-off.

The aircraft's livery was the standard Boeing bright orange floral pattern and the configuration was three by three economy seats with no business class. The cabin panelling was also the standard white plastic. Everything was new but basic. As there were four of us Mum sat with my brother and sister and I sat across the aisle from my Mum next to a couple of Somali businessmen or officials, all smartly dressed in their suits. The plane quickly filled up and we were ready for the off.

As we taxied to the end of the runway - the plane effectively taxiing to the end and turning back on itself - I looked out for Dad and could see him, the embassy fixer and his Land Rover on the apron. Dad was waving frantically as the aircraft thundered down the runway. The 707, with its four turbojet engines roared as it took off. The plane banked left over the city before turning sharp and heading south towards Kismayo.

As we ascended we passed over the beautiful waters below, trying to spot our favourite beaches before climbing to around 20,000 feet and into the cloud. The country that was home for two years was reduced to mere specks from the sky. The cirrocumulus clouds soon enveloped the plane obscuring our view of the ground below. Mogadishu and Somalia were a distant memory and we were on our way home to the UK via Nairobi. The flight was comparatively smooth and turbulence-free. The rest of our journey was completely uneventful - as it should be - and we transited through Nairobi to the British Airways flight home. The layover in Nairobi, Kenya, was of a few hours at Jomo Kenyatta International Airport. This airport is the largest in Kenya and the busiest in the whole of East Africa. Even though we didn't leave the airport, the main city of Nairobi was miles away from the airport and as we landed all I could see around was the bush and the game park we had visited on a holiday. Somalia was now thousands of miles behind us and soon a memory.

Chapter 15 – Afterword

Somalia left an indelible mark on me and my family. It is hard today to truly articulate the paradox of a country with outstanding natural beauty and great potential and yet at the same time a country that was an extremely complex and, at times, a challenging environment even as an expatriot. Indeed, my childhood experiences of living in Somalia continue to present themselves in my adult life today.

I recall having applied to read Arabic at several universities and hearing back from them all except for Durham University's Centre for Middle Eastern and Islamic Studies (CMEIS). My Headmaster, Michael Vallance, then received a panic telephone call from CMEIS to ask, *"Stephen hasn't made his selection yet? We would like to invite him for an interview with Professor Richard Lawless as soon as possible."* I went up to Durham in early February 1990 and as was customary first had my college interview at Trevelyan College and then my departmental interview with Professor Lawless.

I arrived at the department in darkness and as I opened the daw to CMEIS I was bathed in light. Professor Lawless was so apologetic and welcomed me into the department on Elvet Hill. Immediately the conversation ceased to be about my desire to read Arabic and switched to Somalia….! He then spent our entire interview talking about Somalia, tribalism, the camel trade and migration as he was writing an academic paper on migration. Three to four thousand Yemenis, some of Somali heritage, had settled over a hundred years ago in the North East of England, in South Shields, when Aden a British Protectorate and a key bunker port for commercial shipping and Tyneside was an important maritime hub. Professor Lawless clearly was very appreciative of my input! Needless to say, on return home, I received an offer from Durham that was attractive with a note of thanks about our chat on Somalia and how helpful the conversation was. It felt like an entirely natural decision to select Durham to do my degree and candidly have never looked back.

My Somali reference is defined by my childhood experiences of living in a united country ruled by a dictator where there was no opposition, no alternate view and limited freedom of expression. A dictator that was trained by the British, Italians and Russians brought the country out of colonialism and established a Communist-leaning security state. A dictator that destroyed all references to clans – perhaps the most potent force in Somalia – and had a very, very effective internal security service that routed out any opposition. It is sometimes said that the larger your security apparatus, the weaker your government's foundation, which is perhaps why things fell apart in Somalia in dramatic style.

Somalia had the early shoots of civil unrest at the beginning of the 1980s and by the beginning of the 1990s this intensified into all out civil war. The United Somali Congress (USC) rebels had toppled Siad Barre, capturing most villages and towns of Mogadishu. The rebels grew stronger with each passing day defeating Barre's Red Beret special forces. The loss of the government's hold was further weakened when the rest of the rebel groups declined to join hands with the USC rebels. It started another war within the rebellious groups and succeeded by Siad Barre's ousting from the Somalian parliament. These rebellions fought for influence in the created power vacuum and groups clashed to gain control over the capital.

Somalia was racked by civil strife with many citizens now starving to death. The purpose of this operation was to settle down things in Somalia and create favourable conditions for aiding the Somali population in need of food in the southern region of this nation. The alliance was entrusted with ensuring security up until humanitarian operations to stabilize the situation were handed over to the UN and formed the Unified Task Force (UNITAF). The United Nations Operation in Somalia II (UNOSOM II), which lasted for two years, was mostly launched in the south after the peacekeeping coalition's 1993 landing. The initial UNITAF mission statement called for using "all necessary means" to ensure the provision of humanitarian assistance.

On the 9th of December 1992, the US-led UN intervention code-named Operation Restore Hope unfolded on our TV screens when 1,800 US Marines from Camp Pendleton swept ashore just to the south of Mogadishu.

I recall watching the landing in my university college television room wondering if the Marines had landed on Jazeerah Beach or their favourite beach a few kilometres further south, but then I was equally surprised by the awaiting news camera crew! Whilst I am sure done with a high level of coordination with CNN and the US Government, the Marines looked very displeased to be greeted by cameras on prime-time television. It marked a turning point in what we really know now as live television news from a front line or conflict zone.

The Pakistani component of UNOSOM II lost 25 of its peacekeepers on the 5th June 1993, in a conflict with Somali militants making it the worst day for UN forces. The killing of civilians by peacekeepers on the 12th and 13th June heightened Somalians' hostility toward UNOSOM II. Many U.N. officials and diplomats were horrified by the sight of Somali civilians being shot at point-blank range by UNOSOM troops and many saw this as a serious setback to the organization's reputation as a force for peace among the Somali people. After numerous Pakistani soldiers were killed, the Security Council issued Resolution 837, instructing the allied forces to take all necessary actions to bring humanitarian supplies to the Somali people in accordance with Chapter VII of the United Nations Charter. This operation was effective.

Following the Civil War Somalia effectively became a failed state and extremism in the form of Al Shabaab filled the vacuum. What has prevailed until recently has been sheer hell and carnage for the people. There are a number of excellent books that document this period and I leave it to them to speak to the horrendous atrocities and death that has stained the country's history.

Here we are in 2023, and I frequently ponder the question, *'What does the future hold for Somalia?'* That has been an immutable question ever since things started to fall apart in the early 1990s.

To quote Winston Churchill, *"The longer you can look back, the further forward you can look."* I have a strong sense that in 2023 Somalia is now emerging and recognises its strategic importance on the Indian Ocean and to the south of the Middle East. We see Somalia retaking ground from Al Shabaab and displacing the enemy. We see the functioning of a democratic government. And we see the emergence of Somali self-sufficiency and truly understanding its place in the world. A Somalia built by Somalis for Somalis and not one prescribed or designed by a foreign power.

This is despite the terrible natural disasters (drought and flooding) that cause so much human distraction, the ever-present scourge of Al Shabaab and their continued cowardly attacks, and the omnipresent tensions between notions of regional independence, clannism, disputed areas and federalism. Sadly in all, it is the ordinary Somali that suffers at every turn.

In my view, people are quick to criticise the country's progress. If we look far enough back, again to reference Winston Churchill, we see a country and region that dominated the Indian Ocean. Regional trade was controlled in the Middle Ages out of the ports of the Mogadishu Sultanate and the Ajuran Sultanate, centred around the port of Mogadishu but also Barawe and, for me personally, the jewel in the crown Merka. Significant trade was conducted across the Indian Ocean with India and China.

Somalia has immense natural wealth both on land and at sea, and it is strategically key as an entry point to the Red Sea and has the longest coastline in Africa at just over 3,000 kilometres. What it also has is a proud and capable people.

My heart lifted recently when watching a new 10-series Somali TV programme called *Arday*, meaning Student. This series really breaks taboos and delves into topics such as forced marriage, violence and drug use. Whilst the topics are arguably heavy, who would have believed such a programme would have possibly been created?

In 2023 I am very optimistic about Somalia's ability to define itself in a way that brings peace and prosperity and establishes the Rule of Law across its territory. I look forward to the day I can bathe in the most special waters of Jazeerah. Whilst this book looks back to a moment in time in the past, there is much to celebrate and be optimistic about as we look forward.

Perhaps the most positive news of 2023 is the launch of the Somali ID card under the auspices of the National Identification and Registration Authority (NIRA). The objective is to have approximately 15 million people, including children, registered on the new ID card system by 2026. This is a fantastic step and follows many similar schemes adopted by other countries, such as NADRA in Pakistan, to seriously get a grip on terrorism. Indeed, it was NADRA that in 2017 initially entered into discussions with the Somali federal government about the introduction of an ID card system as a key measure in their fight against terrorism.

The ID card system will be essential to undertake any civil activity, including driving licenses and vehicle registration, accessing government provided services eg healthcare, voting, banking, paying taxes, etc. The system operates on the basis of a 'single source of truth' (SSOT) or 'single point of truth' (SPOT) database, which superficially might sound authoritarian, but where any law-abiding citizen has nothing to fear and can live freely. A significant benefit is that it severely restricts the terrorists ability to freely operate in the country. This is a hugely important step for Somalia and an inflection point in their battle against Al Shabaab. The sooner that the ID card system is rolled out the better it will be for the population.

So, despite the challenging environment, living in Somalia paid back. In fairness, it probably has been there all my life and gave me the self-reliance and strength to tackle any obstacle that confronted me. Whilst living in Somalia in the early 1980s was by no means easy, we did exactly as my Mum said we would: *we made the very best of the situation*. We adapted, and we immersed ourselves in the environment and culture. It is my sincerely hope that one day I can return to the beaches of Jazeerah and bathe in its beautiful waters in a democratic and prosperous country free of terror.

Nin ann dhul marini dhaayo maleh

~ He who has not travelled has no understanding.

Jomo Kenyatta International Airport September 2019

Selected Bibliography

The reality is that there are very few books written about Somalia during President Siad Barre's time in power, namely from the late 1960s through to the early 1990s. More recently (in the last twenty years), there are certainly many more books written on Somalia but naturally focused on the demise of the country, the Civil War, continued fractional conflict, and its struggles with terrorism. In my humble opinion whilst these are all well written and factually correct, they are not particularly uplifting and don't celebrate Somalia's rich heritage and culture.

Older works include one of my favourite books on Somalia by Gerald Hanley, *Warriors and Survivors,* written about his experiences in East Africa during World War Two, where he served in the Kings African Rifles (KAR). The book was published in 1971 over twenty-five years after the war finished and forty years since Hanley first went to East Africa in 1934, aged 19. *Warriors and Survivors* is based on Hanley's reminiscences of a time past - perhaps not too dissimilar to my own approach in writing this book. *Warriors*, the first part of his book, has subsequently been republished by Eland entitled *Warriors: Life and Death Among the Somalis* in 1993.

What I like about Hanley's book is its clarity about the sheer remoteness, solitude and harshness of the environment in which ordinary people live. In part it is a Somalia I remember. Hanley's role in the KAR at the time was primarily to keep the peace and prevent bloodshed between feuding tribes. Despite the challenging environment, the Irishman finds humour in his surroundings and again I can relate to that.

Despite my positive view of Hanley's book, many will be critical because it was written by someone with a white, European, and middle-class perspective, and some may incorrectly draw an opinion that the book is a colonialist view of Africa and tribalism. I have read many less-than-positive reviews that describe him as an 'Orientalist' and a racist. If anything, to quote his obituary in The Independent, Hanley had *"a strong conviction that so-called Western 'civilisers' often brought insensitivity and arrogance in their well-meaning luggage"*. From my experience I am sure much of what Hanley wrote is absolutely marked by his perspective set at a point in time and now antiquated. Antiquated, yes, but not racist.

Ernest Hemingway described Hanley as *"The foremost writer of his generation"*, which is high praise indeed. Similar high praise from a more recent travel writer, historian and journalist Justin Marozzi who describes Hanley's Warrior as *"one of the most remarkable accounts in English of this fiery country and her extraordinary people"*. For me, this book is the reference by which all books on Somalia are set.

Professor Ioan Lewis's *Understanding Somalia: Guide to Culture, History, and Social Institutions,* originally published in 1955, is considered the authority on Somali political history. The book provides a detailed context of Somalia before the partition between Somalia and Somaliland and the complexities of Somali society and culture that precipitated what followed. The book also has excellent black-and-white photographs, which in an instant portray Somalia at a point in time. The book is well worth reading and provides an important political context and introduction to a complex environment. Lewis subsequently wrote *A Modern History of the Somali: Nation and State in the Horn of Africa*, which brings his earlier book up to date and addresses developments in the Somali political region since the country imploded in 1991.

Another book well worth reading is Andrew Harding's *The Mayor of Mogadishu*. The book tells the story of Mohammed Nur ('Tarzan') and his family living through Somalia's turmoil, exodus to London, and then subsequent return to Mogadishu as mayor in 2010 when the city was largely under the control of Al Shabaab. The book is well-written and speaks to the turmoil of the city through a biographical account.

I would be remiss in not mentioning Mary Harper. Harper has written two excellent books on *Somalia, Everything You Have Told Me Is True: The Many Faces of Al Shabaab* and *Getting Somalia Wrong?: Faith, War and Hope in a Shattered State*. Both provide a vivid account of perhaps the darker side of Somalia's near-term history. Harper does an excellent job of providing insight into the complexity of the near-term environment.

Somali author and Voice of America journalist Harun Maruf, in partnership with Dan Joseph, wrote a book entitled *Inside Al-Shabaab: The Secret History of Al-Qaeda's Most Powerful Ally*. Again, a well-researched, written and powerful account of the dark side of Somalia's near-term history, including a lot of rich detail on the war fighting on the streets of Mogadishu. A gem for students and practitioners of counter-terrorism.

These books written by Harper and Maruf, whilst perhaps focusing on the more negative side of Somalia's recent history, are essential reading to provide the most up-to-date political and security context. They also perhaps explain the ills of the past in terms of suppression of the most potent of forces in Somali culture- clannism or *qabiilism*. I can certainly relate to Harper and Maruf's books, but they are a million miles from a Somalia I grew up knowing.

One of my favourite books on Somalia is not a novel or reminiscence but something considerably more factual. The book, or rather I should say handbook is by Harold Nelson called *Somalia: A Country Study.* It was published by the US Federal Government in 1982 and edited by Helen Chapin Metz in 1992. The book provides an excellent summary of the political landscape, the economy, society, its organisational structure and national security. The book is a collaboration effort by a number of authors led by Nelson but provides excellent insights and lots of data and details. Whilst this book is not on a par with Hanley's *Warriors,* it is nonetheless important and helps provide context and factual information to a complex environment.

These books provide a comprehensive range of perspectives on Somalia, covering topics such as its history, politics, conflicts, culture and society. They offer insights into the challenges the country has faced and the complex dynamics that have shaped its recent history. The only downside - in the author's view - is that recent literature on Somali perhaps, and understandably so, weighs on the more negative aspects of events over the past 30 years. There is so much to be positive about in Somalia and such a rich history and culture to draw on. Yes, much of it has been destroyed, but part of the process of reconciliation and reconstruction is not just in buildings but rediscovering the country's long history and culture.

Abdi Elmi, Afyare & Osman, Madina M., 'Understanding the Somalia Conflagration: Identity, Political Islam, and Peacebuilding', 2010.

Bowden, Mark, 'Black Hawk Down: A Story of Modern War', 1999.

Fergusson, James, 'The World's Most Dangerous Place: Inside the Outlaw State of Somalia', 2014.

Guliye, A.Y., Noor, I.M., Bebe, B.O., Kosgey, I.S. 'Role of Camels (Camelus Dromedarius) in the Traditional Lifestyle of Somali Pastoralists in Northern Kenya', 2007.

Hanley, Gerald, 'Warriors: Life and death among the Somalis', 1993.

Harding Andrew, 'The Mayor of Mogadishu', 2016.

Harper, Mary, 'Getting Somalia Wrong?: Faith and War in a Shattered State', 2012.

Harper, Mary, 'Everything You Have Told Me Is True: The Many Faces of Al Shabaab', 2019.

Lewis, Ioan, 'Understanding Somalia: Guide to Culture, History, and Social Institutions', 1993.

Lewis, Ioan, 'A Modern History of the Somali: Nation and State in the Horn of Africa', 2002.

Maruf, Harun, 'Inside Al-Shabaab: The Secret History of Al-Qaeda's Most Powerful Ally', 2018.

Nelson, Harold, 'Somalia: A Country Study', edited by Helen Chapin Metz., 1992.

Rirash, Mohamed Abdillahi, 'Camel Herding and Its Effects on Somali Literature', 1988

Mum on a moonlit "Brits Bay"